Left-Handers Speak Out!

"Right-handers are a bunch
you've seen one, you've see
—Neurosurgeon Dr. Joseph Bogan

"The key to a hockey fight is the first punch. When you're a lefty and they're looking for the right, it helps."
—Wayne Cashman of the Boston Bruins

"It is better to stand on the wrong side of the ball, and hit it right, than to stand on the right side and hit it wrong."
—Motto of the National Association of Left-Handed Golfers

"When you have a right-handed lover and you're lying in bed, it works out very well. . . . It's a perfect fit."
—Penny, age 45, Sociologist and Educator

"I can see the day when a 90-degree angle is known as a 'left' angle; when a moral, virtuous person will be called 'lefteous'; and when a box standing on its bottom will be 'upleft.' "
—Customer at a Westport specialty shop for left-handers, 1977

THE LEFT-HANDER'S GUIDE TO LIFE

Richard Donley knows intimately both the glory and the grief that are part of being left-handed. **Leigh W. Rutledge,** his ambidextrous co-author, is learning to get more in touch with the right side of his brain. Both live in Colorado.

The Left-Hander's Guide to Life

*Leigh W. Rutledge
and Richard Donley*

With Illustrations by James Bennett

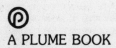
A PLUME BOOK

PLUME
Published by the Penguin Group
Penguin Books USA Inc., 375 Hudson Street,
New York, New York 10014, U.S.A.
Penguin Books Ltd, 27 Wrights Lane, London W8 5TZ, England
Penguin Books Australia Ltd, Ringwood, Victoria, Australia
Penguin Books Canada Ltd, 10 Alcorn Avenue,
Toronto, Ontario, Canada M4V 3B2
Penguin Books (N.Z.) Ltd, 182–190 Wairau Road,
Auckland 10, New Zealand

Penguin Books Ltd, Registered Offices:
Harmondsworth, Middlesex, England

First published by Plume, an imprint of Dutton Signet,
a division of Penguin Books USA Inc.

First Printing, August, 1992
13 12 11 10 9 8 7 6

 REGISTERED TRADEMARK—MARCA REGISTRADA

LIBRARY OF CONGRESS CATALOGING IN PUBLICATION DATA
Rutledge, Leigh W.
  The left-hander's guide to life / Leigh W. Rutledge and Richard Donley.
    p. cm.
  ISBN 0-452-26845-1
  1. Left- and right- handedness—Humor. 2. Life skills—Humor. 3. Ameri-
can wit and humor. I. Donley, Richard. II. Title.
PN6231.L39R87 1992
818'.5402—dc20   92-869
                                                                     CIP

Printed in the United States of America
Set in Souvenir Light
Designed by Eve L. Kirch

To Wibby,
perhaps the most passionately curious
left-hander in the world

CONTENTS

ACKNOWLEDGMENTS

For their help in providing us with information or assistance, we would like to thank Ken Ahrens at the National Association of Left-Handed Golfers, Richard Arnold at *Star Trek: The Next Generation*, Mrs. Mabel Beardsley, Peter Borland, Karen Carlisle, Margaret Cavanaugh, Lisa Colzani, Bill Deane and Pat La Fond at the National Baseball Hall of Fame and Museum, John Diana, Dave Donley, Mike Durbin at the Professional Bowlers Association of America, Mark Finn, Dr. Penny Green, Jacky Griffith, Dr. Suzanne Hetts at the Dumb Friends League of Denver, Thomas Hoffman at Remington Arms, Suzan Ireland at *Lefthander* magazine, Harry Johnson at Polaroid, Stephanie Laidman, Susan Lee, John Logsdon, Jay Manahan at the National Football League, Sharlene McEvoy at Sinistral SIG, Clayton McGraw, Herman Moore at Southpaws International, Bill Neelin at Eastman Kodak, T. Outlaw, Vess Quinlan, Standlee Reid, Edward Rutledge, Dr. Elizabeth Rutledge, Sam Staggs, Paula Susi, Bob Vassar, Susie Watson at Timex, Laurie Weiser, Dr. Fred Yap, and Jimmi Yap.

In particular, we owe an enormous debt to Charlotte Simmons.

1

But Are You Really Left-Handed?

"Who in the world am I? Ah, *that's* the great puzzle!"
—Alice, *Alice's Adventures in Wonderland*

So you thought that just because you pick up a pen and write with one hand or the other, that automatically makes you left- or right-handed? Not necessarily. Maybe that kind of distinction would have passed muster fifty years ago, but in today's world of scientific subtleties and microphysiological distinctions, it's just the beginning. The fact that people use their hands for all kinds of things other than writing—and very few people use one hand or the other for everything they do—means that almost no one is entirely, 100 percent left- or right-handed. Most people fall somewhere along a continuum between the two extremes. It's even possible that someone who has spent a lifetime writing right-handed may in fact be predominantly *left*-handed and may never have even known it. Or vice versa.

So really, the first question is: **Are you actually left-handed?** Or are you just pulling a fast one on Mother Nature?

Over the decades, psychologists, neurologists, even criminologists have come up with a variety of tests and definitions to help pinpoint just exactly who is left-handed and who isn't.

The Torque Test

The "Torque Test" was devised by Dr. Theodore Blau, a clinical psychologist from Tampa, Florida. Draw x's on a page, and then draw circles around the x's, alternating back and forth between your left and right hands with each circle. Note the *direction* in which you draw the circles.

According to Dr. Blau, a person who draws the circles using a counterclockwise motion is predominantly left-handed.

The Thumbnail Test

Hold your thumbs up side by side and look carefully at the nails. According to a study published in *The New England Journal of Medicine*, whichever thumbnail is wider and squarer at the base belongs to your dominant hand. If your left thumbnail is wider and squarer, you're probably left-handed.

The Profile Test

This is regarded by some experts as a highly reliable test of an individual's handedness. Draw the profile of a person's face (or use a dog's profile or that of some other animal—whatever you feel most comfortable with). If, when you're done, the profile you've drawn is facing right, then you're most likely left-handed; if it's facing left, you're probably a natural right-hander.

The Key Tasks Test

Handwriting is one of the most difficult motor control tasks; that's why handedness is largely defined by the hand you write

HAND, EYE, EAR, AND FOOT

Most people have not only a dominant hand, but a dominant eye, a dominant ear, and a dominant foot.

In 1989, a study at the University of Ulster in Northern Ireland found that the vast majority of left-handers consistently hold a phone to the left ear—a seemingly self-evident conclusion, except that it confirmed that most left-handed people are left-ear dominant as well. (And before you start thinking they hold it to the left ear simply because they're left-handed, consider that, in fact, it might be more convenient to hold it to the *right* ear, leaving the left hand free for doodling and taking messages.) Likewise, most—though not all—left-handers are left-eye dominant and left-foot dominant as well.

A minority of people are cross-dominant between hand and eye (that is, they're left-hand dominant but have a dominant *right* eye, or vice versa). Such people, it has been speculated, tend to be more artistic. According to some research, they may also be more prone to insomnia and dizziness.

To determine which eye is your dominant one, extend your arms in front of you and form a triangle by touching your index fingers and thumbs. Visually center an object within the triangle. Close your right eye. If the object stays reasonably centered within the triangle, you are left-eye dominant. If it appears to jump, your right eye is most likely your dominant eye.

with. But check also to see which hand you use to comb your hair, deal cards, strike a match, play golf, pet your dog, open a door, drive screws, and operate your computer "mouse." The Crovitz and Zener Group Test for Assessing Handedness (1962) gave test subjects a list of fourteen actions—including hammering nails, brushing teeth, threading a needle, pouring water from a pitcher, and peeling potatoes—to determine whether each task was usually performed with the left hand, the right hand, or with both hands equally.

If, for example, you write with your right hand but instinctively do almost everything else with your left, it's possible you were born left-handed but were "switched" to right-handed penmanship by a teacher from the "old school" who believed that left-handedness should be drummed out of children.

The Shoelace Test

Believe it or not, there is even a left-handed way ot tying your shoes. Left-handers generally cross first with the left lace on top of the right lace, then form the first loop to the right.

The Happy Face Test

Look carefully at the two faces below. Which of the two is the happy face?

According to some experts, if you chose face #1, you are probably left-handed. If you chose face #2, you are probably right-handed. The two faces are actually mirror images of one another; but the happy side (the side with the upturned lip) is the *left* side on face #1, while the happy side of face #2 is the *right* side.

Tests for Infant Left-Handedness

To test the hand preference of your young child, some pediatricians recommend tossing a ball to the child and seeing which hand he or she instinctively uses to grab it. Or, at meals, place a spoon midway between the left hand and the right hand and watch to see which hand the child uses to pick it up. Although hand preference is not, according to many authorities, definitely established until a child is between three and six years old, there are many early clues. "Don't play to one hand or the other," advises Dr. Jeannine Herron of the University of California at San Francisco, "but allow the preference to emerge naturally."

Keep in mind that when all is said and done, if you *do* write with your left hand, you are entitled to call yourself a left-hander, and no one is apt to argue with you.

How Many Left-Handers Are There?

Estimates of how many left-handed people there are in the world today range anywhere from 5 to 15 percent of the population. The most commonly circulated figure is 10 percent.

A few essential facts about the number of left-handers in the world:

• There are about 50 percent more left-handed males than left-handed females.

• Between 15 and 30 percent of all patients in mental insititutions are left-handed.

• Some experts have claimed that more than a third of all children would be left-handed if they were permitted to demonstrate a natural hand preference on their own, without the interference of parents or teachers.

In the late 1980s, researcher Carol Fry sought to determine whether there was any significant difference in the percentage of left-handers in various college majors at Ohio State University. She found that out of 366 students, a disproportionately high number of left-handers majored in law, while a disproportionately low number majored in microbiology. The final results of her study:

Major	Percent of Left-Handers
Law	21.7
Music theory and composition	19.4
Architecture	17.4
Landscape architecture	15.6
Industrial design	11.4
Accounting	9.3
Microbiology	7.5

Source: Psychological Reports, October 1990.

• While left-handers compose about 10 percent of the general population, they make up almost 20 percent of the high-IQ organization Mensa.

• One curious researcher stood on a city street corner to observe which hand people used to carry their umbrellas. His findings: 80 percent of the people who carried open umbrellas did so with their right hands, while 20 percent carried their umbrellas left-handedly.

One of the peculiarities of left-handedness is that its incidence in the general population seems to decline with age. About 15 percent of all children and teenagers are left-handed. However, for some reason, the ranks of left-handers thin out into adulthood, when only about 7 percent are left-handed. The percentage of left-handers drops even more in the later years: 5 percent or less of all seniors are left-handed.

No one knows for certain why this happens. The most widely publicized—and controversial—theory is that left-handers just don't live as long as right-handers, perhaps as a result of critical injuries sustained in a world primarily designed for right-handed convenience. (Think of all the subtle but significant adjustments a left-hander must make to operate a chain saw or an automobile, for example.) Or it may simply be a reflection of the fact that, up until twenty or thirty years ago, left-handers were routinely "switched" to right-handedness by their parents and teachers.

At any rate, taking most estimates into consideration, there are probably between 20 and 30 million left-handers in the United States alone, and perhaps as many as 550 million left-handers worldwide.

Have Right-Handers Always Been in the Majority?

Some experts say yes, some say no—there's no easy answer to the question.

Studies of prehistoric peoples have at times yielded widely divergent conclusions. A study of Stone Age tools in France found that 55 percent of them were designed for left-handed use. Yet other studies (based on the excavated remains of animals) have claimed that the majority of blows inflicted on animals by prehistoric hunters were struck with the right hand. Some authorities assert that the Neanderthals were, for the most part, ambidextrous; others maintain they were predominantly right-handed; still others contend that the Neanderthal population was about equally divided between left- and right-handers.

In the 1970s, a Canadian team examined more than 12,000 paintings, drawings, and sculptures—dating from 15,000 B.C. to

A.D. 1950—to gauge how left- and right-handedness had been depicted through human populations across the past fifty centuries. In general, the team concluded that human beings have been consistently portrayed as right-handed about 92 percent of the time, from prehistoric eras to the twentieth century.

Meanwhile, there is persuasive evidence that before the influx of European culture, one out of every three native American Indians was left-handed.

A Note on Ambidexterity

During the mid-nineteenth century, British painter Edwin Landseer used to astonish party guests by drawing a deer with his left hand while simultaneously sketching a horse with his right. What particularly amazed people was that both sketches were dramatically detailed, perfectly realistic, and extraordinarily beautiful.

True ambidexterity—that is, the ability to use both hands equally well—is rare. Although many people claim to be ambidextrous, very few actually are. In fact, researchers estimate that only 2 out of every 100 people are ambidextrous—and some experts say that even that figure is too high. (One recent study put the figure at one-third of one percent.)

What many people really mean when they say they're ambidextrous is that they do some important tasks with their nondominant hand: a left-hander may deal cards or catch a ball with the right hand, and a right-hander may tie shoes or cut a steak with the left.

Left-handers *tend* more toward ambidexterity for obvious reasons: it's primarily a right-handed world, and left-handers must learn to adapt to right-handed tools, gadgets, and machinery at an early age. Far more than right-handers, they learn to use both of their hands to some degree.

Interest in ambidexterity (What causes it? Can it be "taught"? Is the tendency inherited?) has increased in the past several years, especially since it has numerous obvious advantages in

professional sports (witness basketball player Larry Bird and tennis pro Luke Jensen).

One of the most celebrated ambidextrous individuals of modern times is tennis champion Martina Navratilova. Navratilova started out writing left-handed—just like her mother—but because she kept getting ink smears all over her writing hand, a teacher suggested she try writing with her right hand instead. She did—and found, to her surprise, that it came as naturally as left-handed writing. She has told interviewers that, much of the time and while engaged in a wide variety of activities. it just doesn't occur to her to favor one hand over the other. She has won more than 1,300 singles matches, including nine Wimbledon titles.

EVERYBODY GOES TO "LEFTY'S"

There's one in almost every city in the United States: a "Lefty's Bar and Grill," a "Lefty's Motor Shop," a "Lefty's Bike Repair." "When we were kids," talk-show host Larry King once remarked, "we all admired 'Lefty.' " For some, the nickname stuck, as illustrated by a sampling of businesses across the country:

Lefty's Storage (Philadelphia)
Lefty's Cigar Store (Pittsburgh)
Lefty's Electrical and Refrigeration (Albuquerque)
Lefty's Welding (Detroit)
Lefty's Cocktail Lounge (Washington, D.C.)
Lefty's Moving Service (New Orleans)
Lefty's Barber Shop (Kansas City)
Lefty's Tavern (Cincinnati)
Lefty's Automotive (Chicago)
Lefty's Bar (Oklahoma City)
Lefty's Auto Electric (Phoenix)

2

Good News and Bad News: A Gallery of Famous (and Infamous) Southpaws

Every year, some half-million new left-handers are born into the United States; hundreds of thousands of them are born into the world each day. If the past is any indication, an usually large number may achieve renown as artists, architects, singers, entertainers, or even outlaws. With that in mind, it should be obvious that a complete list of all the famous left-handers in history would stretch the binding of almost any book to the breaking point. The 199 left-handed or ambidextrous celebrities listed below are just a sampling, and were chosen to reflect a wide diversity of fields, endeavors, personalities, and destinies.

199 Famous Left-Handed or Ambidextrous People

Criminals

William Bonney (1859–1881), "Billy the Kid"
Albert DeSalvo (1931–1973), "The Boston Strangler"
John Dillinger (1902–1934), U.S. bank robber

Elizabeth II

John Wesley Hardin (1853–1895), U.S. gunslinger
Jack the Ripper (flourished 1888), British serial killer

World Leaders

Alexander the Great (356–323 B.C.), Macedonian conqueror
Napoléon Bonaparte (1769–1821), French emperor
Fidel Castro (b. 1926), Cuban dictator
Charlemagne (742–814), emperor of the Holy Roman Empire
Edward III (1312–1377), king of England
Elizabeth II (b. 1926), queen of England
George II (1683–1760), king of England
George VI (1895–1952), king of England
Joan of Arc (ca. 1412–1431), French national heroine

Louis XVI (1754–1793), king of France
Ramses II (13th century B.C.), Egyptian pharaoh
Tiberius (42 B.C.—A.D. 37), Roman emperor
Victoria (1819–1901), queen of England

Artists

Cecil Beaton (1904–1980), English photographer and costume designer
M. C. Escher (1898–1972), Dutch artist
Paul Klee (1879–1940), Swiss artist
Leonardo da Vinci (1452–1519), Italian artist and scientist
Michelangelo (1475–1564), Italian painter and sculptor
Pablo Picasso (1881–1973), Spanish painter
Raphael (1483–1520), Italian painter

Cartoonists

Cathy Guisewite (b. 1950), U.S. cartoonist
Bill Mauldin (b. 1921), U.S. cartoonist
Ronald Searle (b. 1920), English satirical cartoonist

Scientists

Edwin "Buzz" Aldrin (b.. 1930), U.S. astronaut
Alphonse Bertillon (1853–1914), French criminologist
Nicole d'Oresme (1325–1382), French mathematician

U.S. politicians and statesmen

George Bush (b. 1924), U.S. president
Gerald Ford (b. 1913), U.S. president
Benjamin Franklin (1706–1790), U.S. statesman and scientist
James Garfield (1831–1881), U.S. president
Anthony Kennedy (b. 1936), U.S. Supreme Court justice
Robert McNamara (b. 1916), U.S. statesman
Nelson Rockefeller (1908–1979), U.S. vice-president
Harry S Truman (1884–1972), U.S. president

"Back in the seventies, we chose James Michener as one of our 'Southpaws of the Year.' We were working from a list that had been provided to us. Several newspapers carried reports of our selections, and shortly afterward I got a call from a reporter in Austin, Texas. He said he had just spoken to James Michener. And Michener told him that the only thing he does with his left hand is occasionally scratch his right elbow."

> —Herman Moore (founder of Southpaws International) on James Michener, who frequently shows up on lists of famous left-handers

Writers and Journalists

Dave Barry (b. 1948), U.S. author and journalist
Peter Benchley (b. 1940), U.S. author
Jim Bishop (1907–1987), U.S. author and journalist
Lewis Carroll (1832–1898), British author
Richard Condon (b. 1915), U.S. novelist
Ted Koppel (b. 1940), U.S. broadcast journalist
Edward R. Murrow (1908–1965), U.S. broadcast journalist
Forrest Sawyer (b. 1949), U.S. broadcast journalist
Mark Twain (1835–1910), U.S. author

Classical Composers

Carl Philipp Emanuel Bach (1714–1788), German composer
Sergei Rachmaninoff (1873–1943), Russian composer and pianist

Singers, Songwriters, and Musicians

David Byrne (b. 1952), Scottish-born U.S. musician
Glen Campbell (b. 1936), U.S. singer
Phil Collins (b. 1951), British singer and songwriter
Bob Dylan (b. 1941), U.S. singer and songwriter

Sergei Rachmaninoff

Glenn Frey (b. 1948), U.S. singer and songwriter
Eric Gales (b. 1975), U.S. guitarist
Crystal Gayle (b. 1951), U.S. singer
Jimi Hendrix (1942–1970), U.S. guitarist and singer
Melissa Manchester (b. 1951), U..S. singer
Chuck Mangione (b. 1940), U.S. trumpeter
Paul McCartney (b. 1942), British singer and songwriter
George Michael (b. 1953), British pop star
Robert Plant (b. 1948), British singer
Cole Porter (1892–1964), U.S. songwriter
Lou Rawls (b. 1936), U.S. singer
Ringo Starr (b. 1940), British rock star
Paul Williams (b. 1940), U.S. singer and songwriter

Actors and Entertainers

Don Adams (b. 1926), U.S. actor
June Allyson (b. 1917), U.S. actress
Harry Anderson (b. 1952), U.S. actor
Dan Aykroyd (b. 1952), Canadian actor

Robert Blake (b. 1933), U.S. actor
Bruce Boxleitner (b. 1950), U.S. actor
Matthew Broderick (b. 1962), U.S. actor
Carol Burnett (b. 1933), U.S. comedian
George Burns (b. 1896), U.S. entertainer
Ruth Buzzi (b. 1936), U.S. comedian

Sid Caesar (b. 1922), U.S. comedian
Keith Carradine (b. 1950), U.S. actor
Charlie Chaplin (1889–1977), British director, actor, and
    screenwriter
Tom Cruise (b. 1962), U.S. actor

Bruce Davison (b. 1946), U.S. actor
Olivia de Havilland (b. 1916), U.S. actress
Robert De Niro (b. 1943), U.S. actor
Richard Dreyfuss (b. 1947), U.S. actor

W. C. Fields (1879–1946), U.S. comic actor
Peter Fonda (b. 1940), U.S. actor
Allen Funt (b. 1914), U.S. television producer

Greta Garbo (1905–1990), Swedish–U.S. actress
Judy Garland (1922–1969), U.S. singer and actress
Paul Michael Glaser (b. 1943), U.S. actor
Whoopi Goldberg (b. 1949), U.S. actress
Betty Grable (1916–1973), U.S. entertainer
Cary Grant (1904–1986), U.S. actor

Rex Harrison (1908–1990), British actor
Goldie Hawn (b. 1945), U.S. actress

Whoopi Goldberg

Jim Henson (1936–1990), U.S. "Muppets" creator
Rock Hudson (1925–1985), U.S. actor

Danny Kaye (1913–1987), U.S. entertainer
Diane Keaton (b. 1946), U.S. actress

Michael Landon (1936–1991), U.S. actor
Hope Lange (b. 1931), U.S. actress
Cloris Leachman (b. 1926), U.S. actress
Jay Leno (b. 1950), U.S. comedian and talk-show host
David Letterman (b. 1947), U.S. television personality
Hal Linden (b. 1931), U.S. actor
Cleavon Little (b. 1939), U.S. actor

Shirley MacLaine (b. 1934), U.S. actress and author
Howie Mandel (b. 1955), Canadian comedian
Marcel Marceau (b. 1923), French mime
Wink Martindale (b. 1934), U.S. game-show host
Harpo Marx (1888–1964), U.S. entertainer

Andrew McCarthy (b. 1963), U.S. actor
Kristy McNichol (b. 1962), U.S. actress
Steve McQueen (1930–1980), U.S. actor
Anne Meara (b. 1929), U.S. comedian
Marilyn Monroe (1926–1962), U.S. actress

Kim Novak (b. 1933), U.S. actress

Ryan O'Neal (b. 1941), U.S. actor

Bronson Pinchot (b. 1959), U.S. actor
Joe Piscopo (b. 1951), U.S. comedian
Robert Preston (1918–1987), U.S. actor
Richard Pryor (b. 1940), U.S. comedian

Robert Redford (b. 1937), U.S. actor
Don Rickles (b. 1926), U.S. comedian
Julia Roberts (b. 1967), U.S. actress
Mickey Rourke (b. 1956), U.S. actor

Eva Marie Saint (b. 1924), U.S. actress
Telly Savalas (b. 1924), U.S. actor
Christian Slater (b. 1969), U.S. actor
Brent Spiner (b. 1958), U.S. actor
Terence Stamp (b. 1939), British actor

Alan Thicke (b. 1947), Canadian actor

Brenda Vaccaro (b. 1939), U.S. actress
Karen Valentine (b. 1947), U.S. actress
Rudy Vallee (1901–1986), U.S. entertainer
Dick Van Dyke (b. 1925), U.S. actor

Wil Wheaton (b. 1972), U.S. actor
Treat Williams (b. 1951), U.S. actor
Bruce Willis (b. 1955), U.S. actor
William Windom (b. 1923), U.S. actor

> "Bart is trapped in a world where everyone else is struggling to be normal. Bart's response to being normal is 'No way, man!' He is irreverent; he never learns his lesson and is never repentant."
>
> —Cartoonist Matt Groening, on his legendary left-handed cartoon creation, Bart Simpson. Simpson—whose first name is an acronym for "brat," and who was named one of *People* magazine's "25 Most Intriguing People of 1990"—is often forced to stay after school writing contrite sentences such as "I WILL NOT INSTIGATE REVOLUTION" on the blackboard.

Oprah Winfrey (b. 1954), U.S. actress and talk-show host
Joanne Woodward (b. 1930), U.S. actress

Stephanie Zimbalist (b. 1956), U.S. actress

Sports Figures

Earl Anthony (b. 1938), U.S. championship bowler
Larry Bird (b. 1956), U.S. basketball player
Ty Cobb (1886–1961), U.S. baseball player
Jimmy Connors (b. 1952), U.S. tennis champion
James Corbett (1866–1933), U.S. heavyweight boxing champion
Patty Costello (b. 1947), U.S. championship bowler
Dwight F. Davis (1879–1945), U.S. founder of the Davis Cup

Lou Gehrig (1903–1941), U.S. baseball player.
Vernon "Lefty" Gomez (1908–1989), U.S. baseball player
"Lefty" Grove (1900–1975), U.S. baseball player
Dorothy Hamill (1903–1988), U.S. skating champion
Keith Hernandez (b. 1953), U.S. baseball player
Ben Hogan (b. 1912), U.S. golf pro
Carl Hubbell (1903–1988), U.S. baseball player
Reggie Jackson (b. 1946), U.S. baseball player
Bruce Jenner (b. 1949), U.S. decathlon athlete

Sandy Koufax (b. 1935), U.S. baseball player
Tommy Lasorda (b. 1927), U.S. baseball manager
Rod Laver (b. 1938), Australian tennis champion
Greg Louganis (b. 1960), U.S. Olympic diver

Willie McCovey (b. 1938), U.S. baseball player
Stan Musial (b. 1920), U.S. baseball player

Martina Navratilova (b. 1956), Czech–U.S. tennis champion
Manuel Orantes (b. 1948), Spanish tennis champion
Pele (b. 1940), Brazilian soccer player

Brooks Robinson (b. 1937), U.S. baseball player
Bill Russell (b. 1934), U.S. basketball player
Babe Ruth (1895–1948), U.S. baseball player
Vin Scully (b. 1927), U.S. sports broadcaster
Gary Sobers (b. 1936), international cricket champion from
    Barbados
Warren Spahn (b. 1921), U.S. baseball player
Mark Spitz (b. 1950), U.S. Olympic swimmer
Ken Stabler (b. 1945), U.S. football player
Casey Stengel (1891–1975), U.S. baseball manager
Roscoe Tanner (b. 1951), U.S. tennis champion

Fernando Valenzuela (b. 1960), Mexican–U.S. baseball player
Guillermo Vilas (b. 1952), Argentinean tennis champion
Bill Walton (b. 1952), U.S. basketball player
Ted Williams (b. 1918), U.S. baseball player

Miscellaneous

Lord Baden-Powell (1857–1941), founder of the Boy Scouts
F. Lee Bailey (b. 1933), U.S. defense attorney
Josephine de Beauharnais (1763–1814), consort to Napoléon
    Bonaparte
Marie Dionne (1934–1960), one of the Dionne quintuplets
Uri Geller (b. 1946), Israeli psychic
Billy Graham (b. 1918), U.S. evangelist

Helen Keller (1880–1968), U.S. author and advocate for the blind and disabled

Caroline Kennedy (b. 1957), daughter of President John F. Kennedy

Martha Mitchell (1918–1976), U.S. political celebrity

Oliver North (b. 1943), former White House aide

Ron Reagan (b. 1958), son of President Ronald Reagan

Mandy Rice-Davies (b. 1944), British call girl implicated in the Profumo scandal

Renee Richards (b. 1934), U.S. transsexual and tennis player

Norman Schwarzkopf (b. 1934), U.S. general

Albert Schweitzer (1875–1965), French medical missionary

Richard Simmons (b. 1948), U.S. fitness guru

Some Uncommon Left-Handed Individuals

Albert Schweitzer (1875–1965), French Medical Missionary

Schweitzer was an ardent animal lover who acquired a small cat named Sizi during his years in Africa. Sizi developed a habit of falling asleep on Schweitzer's left hand whenever he was sitting at his desk trying to work. The left-handed doctor eventually taught himself to write effectively with his right hand, so as not to disturb the cat.

John Wesley Hardin (1853–1895), U.S. Western Gunslinger

The notorious young outlaw gunned down his first victim—a former slave—when he was fifteen. By the time he was in his early twenties, he had murdered upwards of thirty men, including various other gunslingers eager to test themselves against him. One of his favorite feats involved suddenly crossing his arms and pulling out two Colt .45s—one from each

Albert Schweitzer

side of his vest—and firing them simultaneously, both with lethal accuracy.

M. C. Escher (1898–1972), Dutch Graphic Artist

The famous left-handed artist—renowned for his uncanny and visually provocative creations—attributed his decision to become a graphic artist, rather than a painter, to his left-handedness; he claimed that left-handers were more acute than right-handers as abstract thinkers, and were more likely to be interested in shapes than in colors. One of his most famous lithographs, *Drawing Hands*, portrays a left hand holding a pencil and sketching a right hand; the right hand is, in turn, holding a pencil and sketching the left hand.

Jack the Ripper (Nineteenth Century), British Serial Killer

On the morning of August 31, 1888, forty-two-year-old London prostitute Mary Ann Nicholls was murdered and gruesomely disemboweled on the streets of the city's notorious East End. Her throat was cut from ear to ear, her body was mutilated, and various organs were partially excised. A short time later, a letter (written in red ink) arrived at London's Central News Agency: "I am down on whores and I shant quit ripping them. . . . I love my work and want to start again. . . . Yours Truly, Jack the Ripper." Less than a week later, two more East End prostitutes—forty-five-year-old Elizabeth Stride and forty-three-year-old Catherine Eddowes—were also dead.

From the results of an autopsy on Nicholls's body, officials concluded that the Ripper was left-handed and had probably used a razor-sharp surgical knife to eviscerate her. Those suppositions were later corroborated by the killings of Stride and Eddowes.

In the case of Eddowes, the face and body were savagely, if somewhat extravagantly mutilated, as if the killer had spent a great deal of time "enjoying" himself at his work; her left kidney as well as several other organs, including her uterus, had been removed with surgical precision. (Part of her missing kidney was later mailed to London businessman George Lusk, who was head of a vigilante group formed to solve the Ripper murders. "The other piece," wrote the killer in an accompanying note, "I fried and ate. . . . Was very nice.") Despite their revulsion, investigators were overwhelmed by the expertise with which Eddowes's various organs had been extracted; from that alone, many of them concluded that the murderer must be a seasoned surgeon or physician.

In all, over a period of several months, as many as fourteen women were brutally murdered by the Ripper, though some criminologists set the official figure at six.

Twenty-four-year-old Mary Jane Kelly was murdered in November; parts of her body—including her ears, breasts, and legs—were neatly cut off and then carefully reassembled into bizarre "sculptures." (According to witnesses, Kelly had been seen walking the streets singing "Sweet Violets" just before her disappearance.)

Thirty-five-year-old Martha Turner was stabbed thirty-nine times; the wounds indicated either a left-handed or an ambidextrous assailant.

Forty-seven-year-old Annie Chapman was, like the others, grotesquely mutilated; her kidneys and ovaries had been removed, and her head was nearly severed from her body.

Although the Ripper's identity was never established, persistent rumors suggested that the killer might, in fact, be Queen Victoria's own grandson, the Duke of Clarence, who was, like many members of the royal family, left-handed, and who was known, even to his contemporaries, as a deeply disturbed and sadistic man who frequented street prostitutes. Adding controversy to the case is the fact that many of the papers surrounding the investigation are still sealed under the Official Secrets Act.

Ironically, some good finally came of the murders: their appalling viciousness illuminated the plight of East End slum dwellers and helped initiate a reform movement to improve conditions for the area's orphans, prostitutes, and homeless people. Once regarded as "scum" and "trash," East Enders soon found themselves sympathetically referred to in the press as "those poor unfortunates."

Benjamin Franklin (1706–1790), U.S. Statesman and Inventor

An American da Vinci, Franklin invented bifocals, the lightning rod, and the Franklin stove, wrote the classic *Poor Richard's Almanack*, advanced his century's understanding of electricity, wrote at length on climatology, helped overhaul his fledgling country's educational system, and helped draft and shape the Declaration of Independence (which he later signed). In an essay titled "A Petition to Those Who Have Superintendency of Education," he also sought to eliminate any bias in the nation's schools against left-handedness, noting the turmoil, prejudice, and rebukes that he himself had suffered growing up as a left-hander in a predominantly right-handed world.

Brent Spiner (b. 1958), U.S. Actor

Although well-known for his work on Broadway in such musicals as *Sunday in the Park with George*, Spiner achieved his greatest recognition, starting in 1987, with his often poignant

portrayal of Lieutenant Commander Data on *Star Trek: The Next Generation*. While Spiner is himself left-handed, he portrays the television android as being ambidextrous.

Wil Wheaton, who portrays Wesley Crusher on the show, is also left-handed.

Greg Louganis (b. 1960), U.S. Olympic Diver

A reading disability in grade school—and the subsequent taunts of schoolmates—forced Louganis to seek refuge in gymnastics and dancing, which eventually led to his participation in diving classes as well. Several years later, the left-handed young athlete went on to win two gold medals for diving at the 1984 summer Olympics in Los Angeles, and in 1988 he won two more medals in Seoul. "I picked up some *fabulous* jewelry over there," he said, flashing his medals to an appreciative audience back in the United States. He also received the U.S. Olympic Committee's 1988 Olympic Spirit Award. He has been widely hailed as the greatest diver in the history of the sport.

Gerald Ford (b. 1913), U.S. President

Leaving the White House for a skiing vacation one Christmas, President Ford became so entangled in his dogs' leashes that he nearly fell over. "Merry Christmas," he shouted to the press, "and a Merry—uh—a Happy New Year!" During his three-year stint as the country's chief executive, Ford was seen stumbling down rampways, hitting his head on the sides of swimming pools, and generally knocking things over, all of which led to his acquiring various nicknames in the press, including "President Klutz," "Mr. Ten Thumbs," and "Old Bungle Foot." His notorious clumsiness spawned a continuing series of satiric skits (featuring Chevy Chase) on *Saturday Night Live*, and one columnist mused that Ford might very well become "the first president to be laughed out of office." Said Ford philosophically in his own defense, "You have to expect the bitter and sweet and take a little kidding and let the press and other people get in a few barbs and let it roll off your back like water off a duck's back."

"We used to say jokingly that he even thought left-handed," one of his former high school friends told reporters.

John Sholto Douglas (1844–1900), English Nobleman

The left-handed Douglas helped formulate the famous Marquis of Queensberry rules of boxing and was himself an amateur athlete and pugilist. He was also renowned in his time as a thoroughly disagreeable and bellicose man, having physically attacked numerous people—including one of his own sons, Percy—in public. He was obsessed with what he regarded as effeminacy or weakness of any sort, and when he learned that another son, Lord Alfred Douglas, was having a relationship with Oscar Wilde, he went into a frenzy, threatened to kill them both, and hired thugs to stalk the pair all over England. It was his public accusation of Wilde's homosexuality that eventually led to the playwright's conviction and imprisonment for two years' hard labor on charges of "indecency"—an imprisonment that destroyed both Wilde's physical health and his creativity, leaving him a broken man. It is as much for having precipitated Wilde's

THE LEFT-HANDER'S GUIDE TO LIFE

ruin as for having helped develop the Queensberry rules that Douglas is remembered today.

Victoria (1819–1901), Queen of England

A natural left-hander, Victoria was switched to right-handed penmanship as a child, and she soon became noted for—among other things—her idiosyncratic handwriting, which was euphemistically characterized by one contemporary as employing "much freedom." A later biographer wryly noted that as the queen got older, "The freedom increased while the legibility declined."

Alphonse Bertillon (1853–1914), French Criminologist

In the case of French criminologist and author Alphonse Bertillon, illegible penmanship led to marriage. The left-handed criminologist—whose handwriting was once described as "horrifying"—had to hire a full-time secretary just to recopy his manuscripts before they could be submitted to the publisher. Amelie Notar, the Austrian girl who took the position, eventually became Mme. Bertillon.

Cloris Leachman (b. 1926), U.S. Actress

Not all left-handers have indecipherable handwriting, and not everyone with bad penmanship is left-handed. Still, the two traits sometimes seem to go hand in hand, and like many left-handers, the Oscar-winning actress was no stranger to less-than-satisfactory penmanship grades in school. "In those days," she later told a magazine, "I would smudge everything as I'd write. I still have to sign autographs with my hand up in the air like the body of a tarantula."

Martha Mitchell (1918–1976), U.S. Political Celebrity

The outspoken wife of disgraced U.S. Attorney General John Mitchell was dyslexic and frequently lapsed into stuttering when confronted with an emotional situation.

DYSLEXIA

Generally speaking, dyslexia is a reading disorder associated with an inability to interpret letters and words and to integrate their meaning. It often manifests itself as a tendency to read words backward or to confuse certain letters, such as *b* and *d*, or numbers, such as 6 and 9. However, no definition can evoke the syndrome as vividly as the following graphic description from noted science-fiction writer—and dyslexic—Samuel R. Delany:

"Imagine looking at a page—but the page is on a turntable, spinning slowly before you. And while it's turning, each word on the page is on its own small turn-table, turning in different directions. Then, on top of those one-word turntables, each letter in each word is on a separate turn-table. All of them are turning at different speeds, now changing directions, now changing back again, some getting faster, some getting slower. . . . That is what the ordinary page feels like for the young dyslexic."

Not all dyslexics are left-handed, but the two traits are often linked. In fact, it's been estimated that left-handers are eleven times more likely to be dyslexic than right-handers. Some, but not all, dyslexia may be related to attempts to "switch" a left-handed child to right-handedness. However, the exact cause of the syndrome is still open to controversy, with an increasing number of experts maintaining that it has a neurophysiological basis, and still others claiming it stems largely from mental or emotional conflicts.

Because of the problems dyslexics have with reading, it is often assumed that they are stupid or illiterate. There is, however, absolutely no link between dyslexia and low intelligence, or between dyslexia and illiteracy, as witnessed by even a brief list of some famous people who struggled with it: Virginia Woolf, F. Scott Fitzgerald, Gustave Flaubert, and William Butler Yeats.

Despite her intelligence and extraordinary memory as a child, her parents refused to leave well enough alone and employed rigorous measures to break her of her left-handedness: at dinner, her left hand was tied behind her back, and if she refused to eat with her right, she went hungry. Similar measures were used at school. "Here I was, just a child," she said later. "It made me feel like an outcast; I developed a horrible sense of insecurity and an inferiority complex."

In the late 1960s and early 1970s, she achieved national prominence for her outspoken views on peace protesters, Watergate, and the Nixon administration, as well as for her frequent—and widely reported—verbal gaffes. (She tended to say "embellished" instead of "abolished," and "alleviate" instead of "eliminate"—often lending bizarre, unintended meanings to some of her public remarks.) Her penchant for mixing up telephone numbers became legendary in Washington, and it wasn't uncommon for total strangers to suddenly find themselves talking at length with the wife of the U.S. attorney general: often, having dialed a wrong number, Martha was so flustered and embarrassed she'd stay on the line and chat for a while with whomever she'd called.

Jim Henson (1936–1990), U.S. Puppeteer

Henson achieved wealth and fame in the 1970s and 1980s with his enormously popular Muppet characters. Ironically, he had never intended to become a professional puppeteer. "I mean, it didn't seem to be the sort of thing a grown man works at for a living," he once told an interviewer. One of the earliest and most popular Muppets was the lovelorn, banjo-strumming amphibian Kermit the Frog, who eventually became a kind of alter ego for the low-key and essentially introverted Henson. Kermit was, like his creator, left-handed.

Bruce Willis (b. 1955), U.S. Actor

The left-handed star of the movie *Die Hard* and the once-popular TV series *Moonlighting* suffered from mild dyslexia and a severe stutter as a boy. The stammer eventually helped decide his

WAS EINSTEIN LEFT-HANDED?

Albert Einstein wrote with his right hand and played the violin right-handed (he was a passionate amateur violinist), yet he frequently shows up on lists of famous left-handers. The reason is simple: he exhibited many of the key characteristics of a "switched" left-hander.

Einstein grew up in a Germany that abhorred nonconformity. That abhorrence extended to the classroom, where any and all measures were used to "convert" left-handed pupils. Was Einstein one of these? Some modern researchers think so.

For one thing, Einstein didn't even learn to speak until an unusually late age; by the time he was nine, he still wasn't very articulate. For another, he was, in his early years, such a slow learner that his parents feared he might be mentally retarded. ("He'll never make a success of anything," one of his teachers told his parents.)

Several of Einstein's biographers—chief among them Ronald Clark—have refuted suggestions that Einstein was in any way dyslexic. Instead, they tend to attribute his early slowness to a generally taciturn nature and to the fact that he was painfully bored in the German public schools. Besides, they point out, how could a boy possibly be dyslexic who read Darwin and Kant at thirteen and understood them both better than most adults do?

The puzzle of Einstein's natural handedness will probably never be solved. Still, there are some intriguing questions. For example, Einstein *was* apparently left-eye dominant: photographs consistently show him looking through telescopes and microscopes with his left eye. The odds favor the supposition that if he was left-eyed, he was left-handed as well. Or was Einstein simply "cross-dominant"—that is, right-handed but left-eyed? Such individuals are sometimes said to be more creative, especially when it comes to using their spatial sense and visualizing difficult concepts—two things at which Einstein undeniably excelled.

fate: in school, he discovered that it would mysteriously disappear whenever he got up and performed in front of an audience.

George Michael (b. 1953), British Pop Star

The British pop idol was, in his youth, not only nearsighted and color-blind (as well as left-handed), but overweight, extremely awkward, and introverted—all of which left him with a deep sense of inferiority and confusion. Later he acknowledged, "The whole idea of being a physically attractive personality never really occurred to me"—an astonishing confession from a singer who went on to be ranked consistently as one of the sexiest men in rock and roll.

Paul Wittgenstein (1887–1961), Austrian Pianist

In 1913, Wittgenstein made his debut as a concert pianist, to critical acclaim, in Vienna. Less than a year later he was drafted into the Austrian army. Almost immediately after assignment he was hit by sniper gunfire during a skirmish in Poland. An infection quickly spread in his right arm, and the limb had to be amputated. All hopes of a continued concert career seemed shattered.

During his recovery, Wittgenstein began devoting himself to keyboard exercises to strengthen the muscles and reflexes of his left hand. He also began searching (mostly without success) for left-handed piano works he might one day perform, or for works he could adapt to one hand.

Finally, in 1928, he used some of his family's wealth to commission celebrated French composer Maurice Ravel to write a one-handed piano concerto for him. In 1931, Wittgenstein premiered Ravel's *Concerto in D Major for the Left Hand* to near-ecstatic reviews. Although the actual composition was greeted with somewhat less than enthusiastic comments (several critics expressed serious reservations about it), Wittgenstein himself suddenly emerged as a much-needed figure of inspiration and hope amid the devastation and uncertainty that gripped Europe after World War I. His virtuosity was described as "amazing . . . formidable even for a two-handed pianist." "His physical

LEFT-HANDERS
BY HAPPENSTANCE

Among some of the most famous left-handed people in history are several who, like Paul Wittgenstein, actually started life right-handed, but who, for one reason or another, lost the use of their right hand and became left-handed by necessity. Included in that select group are:

U.S. Senator Robert Dole (b. 1923): Dole became left-handed in 1945 after a combat injury in Italy crippled his right hand.

Hungarian marksman Karoly Takacs (b. 1910): A right-handed sharpshooter who served on the Hungarian Olympic team in 1929 and 1937, Takacs lost his right hand in a grenade accident in 1938. He taught himself to shoot left-handed and went on to win Olympic gold medals in rapid-fire pistol shooting in 1948 and 1952.

Joseph Merrick, "The Elephant Man" (1862–1889): Like most of his body, Merrick's right arm and hand were severely disfigured by neurofibromatosis. By contrast, his left hand remained virtually untouched by the condition, and was in fact quite delicate in size and shape.

English pamphleteer John Stubbes (flourished 1570): In 1579, Stubbes's right hand was chopped off by order of the Crown after he wrote an essay insulting Queen Elizabeth and attacking her policies. He thereafter became left-handed.

Soviet dictator Joseph Stalin (1879–1953): A congenital wasting syndrome made Stalin's right arm increasingly useless with age. He was forced to rely more and more on his left hand.

U.S. concert pianist Gary Graffman (b. 1928): Graffman began experiencing problems with his right hand after he sprained it during a 1967 concert in Berlin. By 1979, it had become severely disabled, and he was no longer able to use it. He has kept his concert career going with performances of Ravel's *Concerto for the Left Hand*, as well as other "left-handed" piano works.

U.S. baseball player Pete Gray (b. 1917): When Gray was a boy, his right arm had to be amputated just above the elbow after it was crushed under the wheel of a milk truck. Despite his disability, Gray later played for the minor leagues, and in 1945—when ballplayers were in short supply—he became the first and only one-armed player in major-league baseball. He played more than seventy games for the St. Louis Browns, and batted—one-handedly—.218.

British naval commander Lord Nelson (1758–1805): His right elbow was shattered by gunfire during fighting in the Canary Islands in 1797. The entire arm had to be amputated (without anaesthetic) shortly after the accident. "A left-handed Admiral will never again be considered as useful," Nelson wrote, "therefore the sooner I get to a very humble cottage the better." As it turned out, Nelson was still *very* useful to the British navy: he continued to lead ships into battle until he was killed at Trafalgar eight years later.

Scottish historian Thomas Carlyle (1795–1881): Carlyle's right hand became progressively more infirm, often trembling uncontrollably, with advancing age. At first he tried writing with a pencil instead of a pen (for more traction on the paper), but that didn't help. Finally, when he was seventy-five, the hand became completely paralyzed and useless; its deterioration may have been part of the generally violent decline in health he experienced after the death of his wife in 1866. "My old right hand (and also my poor old heart) has grown weary of writing," Carlyle told his brother in 1870. He was forced to dictate letters and other writing to a secretary.

handicap was forgotten," said *The New York Times* after one Wittgenstein performance. "He showed commanding musicianship and played with an aplomb and gusto thrice admirable."

Richard Strauss, Benjamin Britten, and Sergei Prokofiev also eventually composed "left-handed" piano works for Wittgenstein, as did a host of lesser composers who were moved by his courage and talent. Meanwhile, the Ravel concerto slowly established itself as a mainstay of the concert repertoire, a minor masterpiece eagerly performed by a wide variety of concert pianists.

In 1939, Wittgenstein emigrated to the United States and settled in New York City with his wife and children. He taught music there and continued to give occasional concerts and recitals until his death in 1961.

Richard Simmons (b. 1948), U.S. Fitness Guru

The doyen of health and exercise—variously described as "the Pied Piper of Pounds," "the Clown Prince of Fitness," and "the Apostle of Adipose"—has a left-handed father as well as a left-handed brother, and is, in his own words, "a very strict lefthander." "About the only thing I can do with my right hand is wave," he told *Lefthander* magazine in 1991.

Edward III (1312–1377), King of England

Edward's left-handedness wasn't confirmed until six centuries after the fact. In 1953, nearly six hundred years after his death, archeological evidence conclusively showed he had suffered a stroke that paralyzed the left side of his body and rendered it useless in later years. Until then, historians had known only that he had suffered some kind of illness that took away his ability to write. Deductively, it became apparent that the king must have been left-handed.

3

Highlights from the History of Left-Handedness

1470 The Scots-Irish Kerr family produced so many left-handed offspring, it was said they designed all of their castle's staircases to favor left-handed swordsmen and put all right-handed intruders at a disadvantage.

1508 Michelangelo, only thirty-three, began painting the ceiling of the Sistine Chapel for Pope Julius II. The resulting frescoes—which Michelangelo labored at for nearly three years—portrayed Adam as having received life from God through the left hand, and only further enhanced the artist's widespread reputation as *Il divino* ("the Divine One"). It was said that Michelangelo, who was ambidextrous, switched hands back and forth to avoid cramps while painting the ceiling.

1519 Left-handed genius Leonardo da Vinci died in Cloux, France, at the age of sixty-seven. He left behind numerous portfolios full of observations on life, nature, and human anatomy—all written in "mirror writing," a minute backward script that ran from right to left. Said the sixteenth-century Italian art historian Vasari, "He wrote backwards in rude characters, and with the left hand, so that anyone who is not practiced in reading them, cannot understand them." Some of Leonardo's contemporaries speculated that he used the baffling script to conceal potentially heretical thoughts about God and nature.

1604 King James I signed a new law reinforcing previous prohibitions against the practice of witchcraft and demon worship. The act led to the wholesale slaughter of suspected witches all over England; in fact, by the mid-1700s, thousands of people—the vast majority of them women, and many of them left-handed—had been put to death. Left-handedness was often (though inconsistently) regarded as evidence of demonic possession. Likewise, large moles and birthmarks on the left side of the body were interpreted as marks of the Devil.

1660 Scottish linguist Sir Thomas Urquhart, best known for his English translation of the poet Rabelais, died in France. During his lifetime, he had tried to develop what he regarded as the ideal universal language, in which each word, instead of being read from left to right, could be read the same either backward or forward. He died—of apoplexy during a fit of uncontrollable laughter one night—before he could complete the task.

1761 The first mass-scale production of scissors—*right-handed* scissors, hundreds of them—began in England.

1779 A vain, temperamental—and left-handed—young Corsican, Napoléon Bonaparte, entered the military college at Brienne, France, where he soon distinguished himself with, among other things, his utterly illegible penmanship and his total inability to spell any word correctly. "His teachers couldn't decipher his compositions," one of his schoolmates later recalled, "and he himself had trouble re-reading what he had written." Years later, after Napoléon became emperor, his former penmanship teacher applied to him for a government pension. "Ah, so you're the one!" Napoléon reportedly told the old man. "Well, you don't have much to brag about!" Nonetheless, he granted his former instructor a generous pension of 1,200 francs.

1799 The first merry-go-round in the United States was unveiled in Salem, Massachusetts. The new contraption, like almost everything in life, discriminated against left-handers: riders had to reach for the brass ring with their right hands.

1811 The original Siamese twins, Chang and Eng, were born in Siam. The two were bound by a medium-sized bridge of flesh that ran from breastbone to navel, and like all fully developed Siamese twins, one was left-handed, the other right-handed. In time, the two men achieved international fame touring in various circuses and exhibitions. They also eventually married (two non-twin sisters, Sarah and Adelaide Yates) and fathered twenty-one children.

1836 E. W. Lane published his *An Account of the Manners and Customs of the Modern Egyptians*, in which he reported, "Many of the Arabs will not allow the left hand to touch food excepting when the right is maimed. . . . It is a rule with the Muslims to honor the right hand above the left: to use the right hand for all honourable purposes, and the left for actions which, though necessary, are unclean."

1848 Working at his lab in Paris, Louis Pasteur concluded that "handedness" (in everything from molecules to people to celestial bodies) was one of the underlying principles of nature. His discovery came as a result of research into the properties of tartaric acid and racemic acid—which have the same chemical composition, but are mirror images of one another, like a pair of gloves.

1876 Italian psychiatrist Cesare Lombroso, director of the lunatic asylum at Pesaro, published his book *The Delinquent Male*, in which he boldly asserted that men who are left-handed (or who have narrow foreheads or protruding ears) are psychological degenerates prone to crimes of violence. A short time later, he published *The Delinquent Female*, in which he made similar assertions about women.

1880 Western outlaw Billy the Kid took time from other activities to have his picture taken at Fort Sumner, New Mexico. The resulting photograph—widely reproduced in newspapers and books—showed the Kid apparently wearing his holster on the left hip, giving rise to the widespread supposition that he was

A FAMOUS WOODEN LEFT HAND

One-handed Captain Jean Danjou was a revered member of the French Foreign Legion in the mid-nineteenth century. Despite the fact that his left hand was a wooden prosthesis (a considerable handicap in those days), he was renowned for his adventurousness and bravery. In the 1860s, Danjou found himself fighting in Mexico to help defend the ill-fated emperor Maximilian. Suddenly ambushed by nearly two thousand Mexican soldiers at an outpost near Camerone, Danjou and sixty-three of his men were hopelessly outnumbered. However, Danjou rejected Mexican demands that he surrender, and instead he and his fellow legionnaires fought to the death. Danjou's wooden left hand was later recovered by comrades from the site of the massacre and sent back to the Legion's headquarters in Algeria—where it was proudly displayed for decades as a revered symbol of Legionnaire determination and honor.

left-handed. In fact, what most people never realized was that the photograph was a tintype—a reversed image—and the holster was actually on Billy's *right* hip. Whatever the truth about Billy's hand preference, eyewitnesses attested to his deadly precision firing a gun with either hand or, on at least one occasion, firing two pistols at once, one in each hand.

1881 James Garfield became the first left-handed U.S. president. During his brief term of office, Garfield often amused visitors by sitting at his desk and writing classical Greek with his left hand while simultaneously writing Latin with his right. Unfortunately, he was shot four months after his inauguration—by a right-handed assassin who boisterously sang, "I am going to the Lordy, I am so glad!" while ascending the gallows.

1884 The notorious left-handed swindler and confidence man Colonel Alexander Branscom was apprehended in New York City and sentenced to ten years in prison. Branscom—a dapper and irresistibly charming middle-aged Virginian who was missing his right hand (he told people he'd lost it in the Civil War)—posed as a book publisher to bilk unsuspecting advertisers and contractors out of tens of thousands of dollars. His forgeries of checks, letters, and loan agreements were considered flawless. "His expertness with the pen is a marvel," said one police chief, "in view of his being obliged to write with his left hand."

1891 The term "southpaw" was first coined by Chicago sportswriter Charles Seymour to describe left-handed baseball pitchers. Because of the way some old ballparks were situated, pitchers faced west: thus, a left-handed pitcher's pitching arm was to the south.

1892 A twenty-six-year-old left-handed boxing challenger, Jim Corbett, stunned the sports world by defeating champion John Sullivan in a bout in New Orleans. A knockout in the twenty-first round won Corbett the championship—and elicited boos and sneers from the crowd, none of whom had ever seen a boxer bound, dodge, and zigzag around the ring the way Corbett did. Corbett—who had previously earned his living as a bank teller—spent weeks in advance choreographing his footwork for the match. He held the championship until 1897, when he finally lost it to a twenty-four-year-old right-handed challenger, Bob Fitzsimmons, in a bout in Carson City, Nevada. Corbett later went on to establish a successful career for himself as a stage actor.

1895 The world's first ballpoint pen made its appearance on the commercial market. However, its use wasn't generally accepted until almost fifty years later. Though a distinct improvement over fountain pens (with their misangled nibs and messy ink), the early ballpoints still ensured that there would be decades of left-handers with smudged handwriting and stained left hands.

1900 Eighteen-year-old artist Pablo Picasso made his first copper engraving: *El Zurdo* (*"The Left-Hander"*). The work depicted a left-handed picador in action in the bullring. In fact, Picasso had actually drawn the picador as *right*-handed; but, forgetting that the engraving would be reversed during printing, he wound up instead with the picador holding his lance in his left hand. Rather than destroy the plate, Picasso simply changed the title.

1905 British social activist John Jackson founded the Ambidextral Culture Society in London and made a passionate plea for mankind to return to a "pure" state of ambidexterity like the apes he had seen at the London Zoo. "There is no disadvantage, but every advantage, in our being truly ambidextrous!" Jackson wrote in a book devoted to the subject. "Why should not perfect Ambidexterity be possible now? WHY CANNOT MAN BE AMBIDEXTROUS AGAIN?"

1907 Lord Baden-Powell, a former officer and spy of the British army, founded the Boy Scouts after running a trial camp for boys on Brownsea Island off the southern coast of England. A short time later, he adopted the left-handed handshake as the "official" handshake of the organization. It was said that he got the idea from an African tribe whose bravest warriors greeted one another left-handedly. Baden-Powell was himself ambidextrous and became an ardent proponent of John Jackson's Ambidextral Culture Society.

1920 Authorities estimated that only 2 percent of U.S. schoolchildren wrote with their left hands. Fifty years later, the number would increase to about 15 percent.

1931 Soviet composer Sergei Prokofiev completed his *Piano Concerto No. 4*, "For the Left Hand." The work was composed especially for one-armed Austrian pianist Paul Wittgenstein. However, after reviewing the piece, with its unusual melodic structure and unconventional harmonies, Wittgenstein returned the work with his apologies and a note explaining, "Thank you for the concerto, but I don't understand a note of it, and shall not play it." Although the work was eventually premiered with a different pianist, it drew lukewarm reviews and remained for many years the least popular of Prokofiev's five piano concerti.

1936   Left-handed batter Ty Cobb became the first baseball player inducted into the Baseball Hall of Fame.

1945   Harry S Truman became only the second left-handed president in U.S. history.

1946   A twenty-year-old left-handed baseball pitcher from the University of Havana, Fidel Castro, flew to the United States to try out for a place on the Washington Senators baseball team. Castro—who excelled at a wide variety of sports—had previously been voted his country's best all-around school athlete.

However, the Senators turned him down, and he returned to Havana, where he got his law degree and subsequently devoted himself to the overthrow of Cuban president Fulgencio Batista.

1951 England's King George VI—a natural left-hander forced at an early age to write with his right hand—recorded his final Christmas Day address to the nation. Unfortunately, the king was plagued more than usual by his lifelong stammer, and (according to his assistant Michael Barsley, who later wrote the book *Left-Handed People*) it was necessary to heavily edit the tape—deleting all the pauses, hesitations, and mispronunciations—before the speech was coherent enough for broadcast.

1952 A U.S. Army study found that of 6,040 recent recruits, 8.6 percent were left-handed. The Army's surgeon general viewed this as a reflection of the number of left-handers in society as a whole.

1965 Thirty-four-year-old left-hander Albert DeSalvo confessed to being the notorious "Boston Strangler," who had killed thirteen women and sexually assaulted dozens of others between 1962 and 1964. "Hey," he cheerfully told the press, "they even know me in the Soviet Union!" Once in prison, DeSalvo was fond of slipping female visitors a copy of a book about him, with the inscription, "Can't wait to get my hands around your throat."

1967 Guitar virtuoso Jimi Hendrix electrified crowds at the Monterey Pop Festival. He played the guitar not only with his left hand, but with his left elbow, his teeth, his tongue, and, at one point, his groin. He then doused the instrument with lighter fluid and set it aflame onstage. *The New York Times* dubbed him "the black Elvis." He died three years later of complications from drug use.

1968 Falsetto camp singer Tiny Tim—famous for his stringy hair and his androgynous persona—played the ukulele left-handed and sang "Tiptoe Through the Tulips" on the TV show *Rowan and Martin's Laugh-In.*

1969 Left-handed astronaut Edwin "Buzz" Aldrin became the second human being to walk on the moon. Approximately one-fourth of all the Apollo astronauts were left-handed.

1970 New Yorker June Gittleson opened The Left Hand, a small shop in Manhattan devoted to hard-to-find items (cameras, soup ladles, bowling balls, wristwatches, even boomerangs) for left-handed people. Gittleson told the press that not only was she left-handed, but, "I'm also left-eyed, left-footed, and left-eared. My dog isn't here, but I've trained him to shake hands left-handed."

1972 Left-handed U.S. swimmer Mark Spitz became the focus of attention at the otherwise tragedy-marred summer Olympics in Munich. Spitz, a handsome and photogenic dental student from California, had already won two gold medals in 1968 and came to Munich intending to sweep all the events in which he was entered. He was true to his word: not only did he win a record seven gold medals—more than any other individual athlete at a single Olympics—but he broke four world records.

Meanwhile, back in the United States, another left-handed athlete—bowling champion Patty Costello—was named "Female Bowler of the Year" by the American Bowling Congress.

1976 *Lefthander* magazine (originally called *Lefty*) made its debut. Devoted to the interests and needs of southpaws around the world, the magazine was founded by Kansas businessman Dean Campbell, who later organized the first International Left-handers Day on August 13, 1976. Campbell acknowledged that the event was held on the 13th to make fun of all the superstitions surrounding left-handedness.

1976 *Cathy*—a comic strip written by left-handed cartoonist Cathy Guisewite—premiered in sixty newspapers across the country and quickly established itself as one of the most popular comic strips in the nation. The strip features a single, working woman named Cathy, who is also—like her creator—left-handed.

1977 A Huntington, Pennsylvania, woman, Mary Francis Beckley, left $10,000 to nearby Juniata College to be used for scholarships for worthy young students. Her only stipulation was that the recipients of the aid must be left-handed. Beckley and her late husband were themselves both left-handers.

1980 The Riverside, Missouri, police department fired a left-handed officer, "Woody" Winborn, after he refused to wear his gun holster, per tradition, on the right side. Winborn later sued the department and received an out-of-court settlement.

1985 A left-handed supermarket checker in Woodridge, Illinois, won a "left-handed" discrimination suit against the store where she had once worked. The checker, Crystal Sagen, said she had felt compelled to quit her job after repeated clashes with the manager, who insisted she use her right hand—and *only* her right hand—to run groceries over the computerized laser scanners. "It didn't make sense," Sagen said. "It was discrimination against left-handers." She was awarded $136,000 in damages.

1987 The 1988 presidential campaign got under way with an unprecedented one-in-four chance that the next president would be left-handed. Of the twelve presidential candidates, three (all Republicans) were left-handed: Pat Robertson, Robert Dole, and George Bush. Bush was elected several months later, raising— in the words of humorist Dave Barry—"a troublesome constitutional issue, because every time he signs a bill into law he drags his hand through the signature and messes it up."

1990 A study at the Montreal Neurological Institute revealed that while people may vary in which hand, foot, ear, and eye they favor, the right nostril is dominant in all people. The study showed that the right nostril is significantly more effective than the left in discriminating between odors.

1990 Timex Corporation put out its first left-handed watch—the "Lefty"—designed with the stem (for setting the time) on the left side. Price: $27.95.

1991 A study by psychologists Diane Halpern and Stanley Coren concluded that left-handers live an average of nine years less than right-handers, largely as a result of accidents and injuries sustained while trying to function in a predominantly right-handed society. Halpern was later paired off against *Lefthander* magazine editor Suzan Ireland during a segment of *Larry King Live*. "This just seems totally outrageous," Ireland said of the study, while acknowledging that it at least drew attention to the problems of left-handers. The two also began arguing over whether former president Ronald Reagan had been left-handed. "He did certain activities with his left hand," Halpern asserted. "If you watch him waving, for example . . ." "He was not [left-handed]," Ireland maintained, with some emotion. "He wasn't. . . . No, he was not."

4

Manual Training: A Brief Refresher Course in Both Hands

"The slender expressive fingers, forever active . . . came forth and became the piston rods of his machinery of expression."

—Sherwood Anderson, "Hands"

There are thirty-two muscles in each of your hands. Contrary to what you may think, there are no muscles in your fingers—only tendons and bones. The muscles that operate your fingers are located in the forearm and palm. It takes ten muscles to move the thumb, six to eight to move each of the other fingers.

Human beings employ two main kinds of grips with their hands: the power grip and the precision grip. To get an idea of each, just imagine opening a jar. At first you use a power grip to loosen the cap. Once the cap is loosened, your hand instinctively changes to what is called a precision grip to remove it completely.

The average firm handshake—a sort of modified power grip—exerts approximately 90 pounds of pressure, though some over-enthusiastic handshakers may wind up squeezing your hand with as much as 150 pounds of pressure. (Author Margaret Halsey once wrote of an acquaintance, "His handshake ought not to be used except as a tourniquet.")

Look closely at the backs of your hands. In each square inch of skin, there are more than 300 sweat glands, 35 hair follicles, 10 feet of blood vessels, and 9,000 nerve endings.

The tips of your fingers are some of the most sensitive parts of the body: the skin there is packed with an unusually high density of sensory nerve receptors. Some people who are blind develop such a highly refined sense of touch that they are actually able to "read" the letters—just the slight elevation caused by the ink—on a normal page of text.

Of all human hands, the longest on record measured twelve and three-quarters inches from the wrist to the tip of the middle finger, and belonged to modern giant Robert Wadlow (1918–1940), who stood eight feet, eleven inches tall.

The largest known hand span of any human being was that of left-handed composer and pianist Sergei Rachmaninoff, who could cover twelve white keys on the piano with one hand. Rachmaninoff could play a chord of C, E flat, G, C, and G with his left hand.

In most people, the middle finger is by far the longest.

Animals with six digits on each paw are relatively common. A domestic cat with six toes, for example, is not unusual, and even among people the phenomenon is by no means unheard of.

Roughly three out of every thousand people are born with a congenital condition known as *syndactyly*, in which there is webbing between the fingers. The condition is more common among men than among women.

Fingernails are dead tissue composed of a substance called keratin, a protein that is also found in hair, feathers, horns, and beaks. Nails are said to grow slightly faster on the dominant hand. They also grow faster in the summer than in the winter. (Constant nail biting may also spur their growth.) During an average lifetime, each finger will produce approximately twelve feet of nail.

Any serious illness can leave tiny horizontal lines—called "Beau's lines"—on your nails. Even severe emotional disturbances, such as chronic depression, can ruin or have an impact on the nails.

Brittle, cracked nails are often a sign of nutritional deficiencies.

Opaque, white nails may be a sign of liver disease. Separation of the nail from its bed can be an indication of hypothyroidism.

Constantly cold hands can also be a sign of thyroid problems.

What we call fingerprints are actually tiny ridges of flesh, much like the tread on a tire, which improve our ability to grasp and hold objects. Even identical twins do not have the same fingerprints, though at first glance their prints tend to look quite similar; there are, however, minute differences in the ridges.

Fingerprints were first used as a means of identification by the Chinese as early as 200 B.C. Their widespread use in criminal investigations, however, did not come until 1901, when fingerprinting of criminals was officially adopted by Scotland Yard.

The prefix *chiro-* is generally used to indicate any technical terms having to do with the hands. For example, the vast majority of people are *chirognostic*—that is, they can tell their left hand from their right. (There *are* some people with perceptual disabilities who can't.) Handwriting is technically known as *chirography*. And a *chiropractor* is one who practices medicine with the hands.

Palmistry—the art of reading the past and the future through the lines and shapes of the hands—is technically known as *chiromancy*, and may have been practiced as far back as the Stone Age. Aristotle, Napoléon, and Alexandre Dumas all had a fascination with the subject.

Better to study a palm, though, than to eat it: among some aboriginal tribes in Australia, it was common to eat the palm of a slain enemy and thereby supposedly ingest some of his physical prowess.

In 1632, an Italian named Camillo Baldi developed the first principles of graphology: that is, trying to determine people's character traits and personalities from samples of their handwriting. Among some of history's most ardent amateur graphologists were Edgar Allan Poe, Thomas Carlyle, Goethe, and Disraeli.

Some common examples of graphological analysis: a very small capital I may indicate that you have an inferiority complex; handwriting with no slant (leaning neither to the left nor to the right) indicates a cool-headed, often judgmental person; if you do not completely cross your T's, you may be prone to procrastination.

The first widely accepted manual alphabet (sign language) for the hearing-impaired was developed by Charles Michel, Abbé de l'Épée, at his school for the deaf in Paris in the late 1700s. Today, sign language is the fourth most frequently used language in the United States, outranked only by English, Spanish, and Italian.

According to cultural anthropologists, all human beings have a "vocabulary" of literally thousands of hand gestures, each one communicating a nuance of exasperation, affection, frustration, happiness, despair, or amusement. In fact, some researchers believe that the number of expressive hand gestures far exceeds the number of spoken words in our vocabulary.

For whatever reason, some hand gestures seem to transcend time and cultural differences. For example, the ancient Romans called the middle finger *impudicus*—"the shameless finger"—because even then it was frequently used to express derision and annoyance.

5

*Ambidextrous Apes and
Left-Handed Blonds: Clues to
the Causes of Left-Handedness*

"O investigator, do not flatter yourself that you know
the things nature performs for herself."
—Leonardo da Vinci

The origins of left-handedness remain a mystery.

In the fourth century B.C., Plato theorized that all people were
born ambidextrous and that it was only because of "the folly of
our nurses and mothers" that children were pressured into
choosing one hand over the other.

The playwright Aristophanes, a contemporary of Plato, had
his own poetic conjecture: people, he said, were originally created round like apples, with no fronts or backs, no left or right;
Zeus, in a fit of pique one day, split everyone in half, and sided-
ness (as well as the eternal search for our other halves) began.

The quest for an answer to the riddle of left-handedness continued into the Middle Ages, and the theories reflected the times.
Left-handedness was caused by the Devil taking possession of
one's soul. Even a brief encounter with the Devil could suddenly
make one left-handed (and leave moles, warts, and other marks
on the left side of the body).

By the seventeenth century, scientific rationalism had replaced
superstition, and many of the explanations began to acquire
a seductive patina of medical logic. "Experts" laughed at the

imaginative lore of the past—and then calmly asserted that left-handers were simply weak and defective versions of humankind, right-handers being the proper and intended archetype. A lively interest in anatomy also emerged: could left-handedness somehow be related to the internal misalignment of some people's organs and muscles? The "experts" disagreed.

They still disagree today. Although some of the clues to left-handedness are slowly, finally, revealing themselves to researchers and scientists, the essential enigma of why some people are left-handed remains. And the fact is, when all is said and done, different people may be left-handed for different reasons.

Right-Brain, Left-Brain

In order to understand some of the theories about left-handedness, it helps to know a few things about the brain first.

The average human brain weighs almost three pounds (slightly more for males, slightly less for females), contains more than 100 billion neurons, and is divided into two very slightly asymmetrical hemispheres, the left and the right, with a complex mass of nerve fibers—the *corpus callosum*—connecting the two.

The purpose of the corpus callosum—which is, for reasons yet unknown, as much as 11 percent larger in left-handers—seems to be, in part, the facilitation of "communication" between the two hemispheres.

The two hemispheres tend to control different tasks. A vivid example of the way the hemispheres operate can be seen in some stroke victims who, though rendered totally unable to speak, may still be perfectly capable of singing. That's because the left hemisphere of the brain tends to control many of our verbal functions, while our memory for music is usually located in the right hemisphere. This startling phenomenon was well documented as far back as 1754, when a doctor wrote of one of his stroke patients, "He can sing certain hymns, which he had learned before he became ill, as distinctly as any healthy person.

Yet this man cannot say a single word except 'yes.' " A stroke that affected the left hemisphere might weaken or eradicate a person's ability to remember words or speak them, but would leave the ability to sing some of those same words intact.

Other functions sometimes attributed to the right hemisphere include:

spatial sense
depth perception
the ability to recognize faces
the ability to invest speech with meaningful emotional nuances

Functions often attributed to the left hemisphere include:

logic skills
a memory for names
the ability to speak and form coherent sentences
the ability to dissect and analyze difficult concepts

In years past, it's been popular to overdramatize the dichotomy between the left and right hemispheres of the brain. The left hemisphere, it was commonly said, can only analyze things in a rigid, logical, sequential manner (much as a computer does), while the right hemisphere tends to absorb and reflect intuitively on what it sees. ":Getting in touch" with the right side of the brain (allegedly the more mysterious and artistic side) had a certain fashionability for several years.

However, neurologists and brain researchers increasingly tend to view this dichotomy as simplistic and naive. Recent research indicates that brain functions are much more complicated; a proper integration of who we are, our *humanness*, depends on the two hemispheres side by side. And whereas, for example, the left side of the brain may indeed govern verbal abilities in some people, for other people those same abilities may reside in the right hemisphere or be spread in a complex manner across both hemispheres.

"We're trying to understand the most complex piece of matter

FIVE ABANDONED THEORIES
OF LEFT-HANDEDNESS

1. Left-handedness is a willful, neurotic choice made by obstinate and antisocial individuals. Left-handedness, wrote psychiatrist Abram Blau in the 1940s, "is nothing more than an expression of infantile negativism and falls into the same category as ... general perverseness." Left-handers, he added, often come from families in which the mother is cold and inattentive and withholds affection.

2. All people are born right-handed. Some become left-handed because they are mentally or physically deficient and cannot properly learn right-handed skills.

3. Most people become right-handed because their arteries are stronger on the right side of their bodies; therefore, the muscles on the right (including in the right hand) are stronger as well. Left-handers have larger and more efficient arteries on the left side of their bodies.

4. Because the heart was once believed to lie in the left side of the chest, early warriors sought to protect it by carrying their shields with the left hand while holding their clubs and spears in the right. Thus the right hand became the species' active hand and the left became the passive hand. Left-handed individuals are presumably descended from tribe members who rarely took part in fighting and who instead concentrated on agriculture, art, and other peaceful endeavors.

5. Left-handedness is the result of bad toilet training, in which the child becomes confused over which hand should be used for toilet hygiene and which should be used for other tasks.

in the known universe," brain researcher Jerre Levy, of the University of Chicago, has said. "No complex function—music, art or whatever—can be assigned to one hemisphere or the other. Any high-level thinking in a normal person involves constant communication between the two sides of the brain."

"Cross-Wiring"

Human beings are "'cross-wired"—that is, the right hemisphere controls the left side of the body, and the left hemisphere controls the right side of the body.,

Generally speaking, then, the left hand is governed by the *right* hemisphere; the right hand is governed by the *left*—leading to the popular T-shirt and coffee mug slogan:

> "If the right side of the body is
> controlled by the left side of the brain,
> and the left side of the body is controlled
> by the right side of the brain, then
> left-handed people are the only ones
> in their right minds."

Brain Drain or Brain Sprain?

A few years ago, scientists speculated that left-handedness was the result of a difficult or stressful birth, as if natal trauma somehow "sprained" the brain. Doubt was soon cast on that theory, however, when one British researcher found that, of some 12,000 test subjects, no correlation could be found between handedness and birth circumstances.

More recently, scientists have theorized that left-handedness results from a reduced supply of oxygen to the brain just before birth. The left hemisphere is slightly damaged, and the right hemisphere tries to compensate and takes over.

Proponents of this theory point to the high incidence of stammering and dyslexia among left-handers (supposed proof that the left, more verbal hemisphere has been damaged), and to the fact that there are a disproportionate number of left-handers among epileptics and the developmentally disabled. In fact, it has been estimated that 65 percent of all autistic children are left-handed.

A Surge of Hormones

Other researchers maintain that left-handedness is the result of hormone imbalances—specifically, irregularities in the levels of testosterone—in the mother's body during pregnancy. This theoretically causes the right hemisphere of the brain to develop more quickly, thus giving dominance to the left hand.

Although testosterone is primarily known as a male sex hormone, it plays an important role in the fetal development of both sexes, and exerts a powerful influence on the normal development of the fetal brain. Once we have been born and have matured, much higher levels of testosterone can be found in men than women. However, with age those levels gradually decrease in men and increase in women. Given all that, one might expect that older mothers would, on average, have more left-handed children. As it turns out, that's exactly what happens: more left-handers are born to older mothers than to younger mothers.

Birth Order

A 1989 study at St. Lawrence University in Canton, New York, found no correlation between left-handedness and birth order.

Heredity

What role does heredity play in who becomes left-handed and who doesn't?

Even while we're still in the womb, we use our hands: we suck our thumbs. Recent studies indicate that while the majority of fetuses (95 percent) suck their right thumbs, 5 percent prefer to suck the left thumb. This seems to suggest that hand dominance may be determined before environmental factors come into play.

There's more intriguing evidence for the role of heredity:

Two right-handed parents have only a 10 percent chance of producing a left-handed child.

If only the father is left-handed, the odds are still the same: 1 in 10.

If only the mother is left-handed, the odds increase to roughly 1 in 5.

But if both parents are left-handed, there is a staggering 40 to 50 percent chance that the child will also be a left-hander.

Do Left-Handed Blonds Have More Fun?

According to one U.S. study, blonds are twice as likely to be left-handed as brunets and redheads.

Other studies have shown that boys are nearly twice as likely to be left-handed as girls.

And among fraternal twins, there's a disproportionately high incidence of left-handedness, though it's rare that *both* are left-handed.

Right-Handed Rats and Left-Handed Honeysuckle

Humans are not the only living things to demonstrate some level of "handedness."

One study of rats found that about half of them used their right paws with some regularity to press a food lever during experiments, while the other half consistently preferred to use their left paws.

Studies show that certain kinds of primates—galagos (or bush babies) and lemurs, in particular—are overwhelmingly left-handed. In some populations of galagos, the left-handers were found to outnumber the right-handers by nearly nine to one.

Among chimpanzees and gorillas—man's nearest relatives on the evolutionary scale—no preference has been found for one hand over the other, though gorillas' left arms are slightly heavier and more muscular than their right arms, indicating perhaps some slight left-arm bias.

Continuing studies of dogs are so far inconclusive, but indicate that "pawedness" may also exist among canines.

Meanwhile, even plants demonstrate some rudimentary level of "handedness." Most climbing plants twine to the right; however, a small number of others—including honeysuckle—consistently twine to the left instead.

Survival "Programming"

"We're crazy as a species if we try to push everybody through the same cookie mold. . . We're *biologically meant* to be diverse . . . and such diversity is helpful to all of us."

—*Jerre Levy*

The human race is extraordinarily plastic: that is, it incorporates a wide variety of traits and differences (many of them seemingly pointless) that provide a broad foundation of genetic diversity, thus helping to ensure the survival and development of the species.

In the end, regardless of the underlying conditions that promote it, left-handedness may simply turn out to be part of the evolving biological diversity that has been essential to the survival of the human race.

And, whatever the exact *cause* of left-handedness, we have at least seen a shift over the past few decades in the way a growing number of researchers approach the subject: away from a "disease model" approach (such as might be used to investigate such anomalies as cancer, autism, or birth defects) and toward an acceptance of left-handedness as a non-harmful, potentially beneficial variation of human biology.

So Just Exactly Why *Are* You Left-Handed?

The fact is, no one knows.

6

The Ups and Downs, the Highs and Lows, the Joys and Sorrows of Being Left-Handed

"Living backwards!" Alice repeated in great astonishment. "I never heard of such a thing!"
— Alice, *Through the Looking-Glass*

"It's a crying shame that ten percent of the world's population has to go through life backward."
— Left-handed business entrepreneur
Christopher Mills, who started a mail-order
catalog for left-handers in the 1970s

Most left-handed people adjust to "living backwards" at an early age. And a fair number become remarkably ambidextrous in the process. Manual transmissions, measuring cups, power saws, corkscrews, cameras, scissors—almost everything is manufactured with right-handers in mind, and when designers think of convenience, they think of *right-handed* convenience. This of course leaves left-handers inhabiting a world in which almost everything is reversed from the way their bodies tell them it should be.

Tape measures run backward; playing cards, when fanned out, reveal nothing at all (the numbers are all in the opposite corners); vegetable peelers don't peel correctly.

Pants flies open up from the wrong side; screws turn the wrong way; even irons often have their cords hanging from the wrong side so that something as simple as pressing one's clothes can become a logistical quagmire.

HELP IS AT HAND

While neither Polaroid nor Kodak makes cameras for left-handed use, Yashica produces a 35mm single-lens reflex camera specifically designed for left-handers.

And Timex—unlike its closest competitor, Bulova—produces two different models of left-handed watches. (There is also a small specialty line of left-handed timepieces, Karis Watches, available through an outlet in San Francisco.)

Meanwhile, both Panasonic and Fuji have introduced camcorders specifically designed to be as easy and convenient for left-handers to use as right-handers.

Products, tools, and equipment for left-handers can be difficult to find. Left-handed tools—gardening implements, kitchen utensils, household conveniences—are often manufactured in Europe and imported by U.S. distributors.

There are still only a handful of left-handed specialty shops across the country (mostly in the larger metropolitan areas), but a number of mail-order supply companies feature left-handed products and can ship them almost anywhere. A list of these outlets appears in Chapter 11.

One of the few U.S. companies to specifically manufacture left-handed models of its products is Remington Arms Co., Inc. Besides its regular line of firearms, Remington makes several left-handed rifles and shotguns. "The bullets," said a company spokesman, "are of course ambidextrous."

The language runs from left to right (instead of the more comfortable right to left); watches must be set on the right-hand side; even saxophones are designed with right-handed musicians in mind.

When Alice tried to imagine what life was like on the other side of the looking glass, she was imagining the life that most left-handers lead every day.

Even if you're a left-handed pitcher for a major-league team and take home $2.5 million a season, or a left-handed tennis pro soaking up the adulation of your fans, you're still stuck having to open a can of pork and beans with a right-handed can opener. It's not much solace that the everyday obstacles for left-handers come with no malice aforethought: the fact is that the average right-handed person goes through life with scarcely a thought about hand preference one way or the other. The right hand is "the one," the left hand is "the other one"—and the left one gets little thought or attention.

Most left-handed people could make a long list of all the products, tools, and customs that discriminate against them. At the risk of telling left-handers what they may already know from hard experience, even a cursory comparison illustrates how many things come with the built-in potential for making a left-handed existence uncomfortable, if not at times miserable:

Items That Discriminate Against Left-Handers	Items That Are Left-Hander-Friendly
watch stems	typewriters
phone booths	computer keyboards
men's shirts	women's blouses
ice cream scoops	highway tollbooths
decorative belt buckles	
rulers	
voting machines	
chain saws	
power saws	
slot machines	
bowling balls	
pinball machines	
dust mitts	
playing cards	
aprons	
golf clubs	
scythes and sickles	
coffee mugs with imprinted messages	
butter knives	
drinking fountains	

There *are* a few things in life that don't discriminate against either left- or right-handers (Frisbees come to mind), but a large number of everyday objects force most left-handers to work a little harder at life.

Pencil sharpeners, music boxes, and microfilm viewers all have the crank on the right side.

Pocketknives have to be opened with the right thumbnail.

Soup and punch-bowl ladles pour from the wrong side for left-handed use.

Even postage stamps go on the upper *right*-hand corner of

Why do women's blouses button from the left while men's shirts button from the right? The answer goes back many years. Men, it was presumed, tended to dress themselves, whereas wealthy women were often dressed by maids: the left-hand row of buttons on a blouse was more convenient for right-handed servants.

FIVE OF THE TOP-SELLING ITEMS AT "LEFT HAND WORLD"

1. Left-handed scissors
2. Left-handed spiral notebooks
3. Left-handed measuring cups
4. Left-handed corkscrews
5. Left-handed can openers

Courtesy Karen Carlisle, owner of the left-handers' specialty shop Left Hand World in San Francisco—"The Shop Where the Customer Is Not Always Right."

---

the envelope (although, according to the U.S. Postal Service, a letter will probably still go through if the stamp is put on the left).

Admittedly, these things represent minor inconveniences for most left-handers. "I've been a left-hander for eighty-nine years," one woman proudly reported to *Lefthander* magazine, "and managed real well in a right-handed world."

For most left-handed people, the physical, day-to-day obstacles of life seem relatively negligible. Right? *Right?*

Danger on the Left

"You should never pick up a newspaper when you're feeling good, because every newspaper has a special department, called the Bummer Desk, which is responsible for digging up depressing front-page stories with headlines like DOORBELL USE LINKED TO LEUKEMIA and OZONE LAYER COMPLETELY GONE DIRECTLY OVER YOUR HOUSE."

—*Left-Hander Dave Barry*

The notion that the disadvantages faced by left-handers might be more than negligible was first broached many years ago with

LEFT-HANDERS WHO LIVED TO A RIPE OLD AGE

Michelangelo—89	Queen Victoria—82
Harry Truman—88	Jim Bishop—80
Greta Garbo—85	King George II—77
Rudy Vallee—85	Cecil Beaton—76
Benjamin Franklin—84	Harpo Marx—76
Casey Stengel—84	Ty Cobb—75
Cary Grant—84	"Lefty" Grove—75
Rex Harrison—82	Mark Twain—75

studies purporting to show that left-handed children (especially *strongly* left-handed children) were much more prone to allergies and asthma than right-handed children. Similar findings have snowballed through the decades:

• Left-handed children are two to three times more likely to suffer from juvenile diabetes.

• Left-handers, on average, reach puberty four to six months later than right-handers.

• Left-handed adults face a higher than normal incidence of insomnia, migraine headaches, ulcerative colitis, phobias, and manic depression.

• Left-handers are three times more likely to commit suicide than right-handers.

• Left-handers are more sensitive to drugs such as tranquilizers and painkillers.

• Left-handers are more prone to alcoholism.

• Left-handers are 54 percent more likely to be injured using tools and implements, and are 85 percent more likely than right-handers to be injured in automobile accidents.

The alarming statistics reached a crescendo in 1989 when Canadian psychologist Dr. Stanley Coren concluded that left-handers have, on the average, as much as a 2 percent chance of dying younger than right-handers. Then, less than two years later, Coren and a colleague, Dr. Diane Halpern, made national headlines when they announced the results of a study allegedly showing that left-handers live an average of *nine years less* than right-handers. Using death statistics from southern California and following them up with questionnaires to determine whether the deceased were left- or right-handed, they concluded that, due to serious accidents and other problems, left-handers have a significantly lower life expectancy than right-handers: sixty-six years, as compared to seventy-five years for right-handed individuals. The number of left-handers, they claimed, begins to thin out dramatically in older segments of the population.

Their findings were, to say the least, controversial.

Numerous psychologists and researchers objected to Coren and Halpern's methodology, claiming that it was "lax" or "unscientific," or that it didn't properly take into account the fact that left-handers might *seem* to be underrepresented in older segments of the population because older left-handers were more likely to have been "switched" as children.

"It's hard to believe," said Dr. Paul Satz of the University of California at Los Angeles, when asked about the study by *The Los Angeles Times.* "There's very little evidence in clinical medicine where something leads to such a big difference in longevity."

Dr. Halpern, meanwhile, defended the findings: "I know this sounds really crazy . . . unless you happen to know the literature on left-handedness. There is an extensive research literature and we found that in several studies left-handers report more accidents, particularly serious accidents, probably because of the way equipment is designed for optimal use by right-handers." In fact, Halpern and Coren concluded that left-handers were six times more likely to die in accidents than right-handers.

It doesn't seem unreasonable to assume that certain tools—right-handed power saws, lathes, even automobiles—might, by their very design, pose a greater threat to left-handers using them. And it's possible that certain elements of *some* left-handers' perceptual faculties could leave them more vulnerable to certain kinds of accidents. (See the brief interview with "Penny" in Chapter 10, "Left-Handers Speak Out.") But for now , many researchers have begun to challenge not only Coren and Halpern's work, but other previously accepted data linking left-handedness to everything from migraines to suicide. There's a growing belief that all of these findings may need to be reexamined, with a careful eye to inherent biases in the research. (Why, for example, do researchers seem so much more intent on exploring the medical ramifications of left-handedness than those of right-handedness?)

Whatever the results, and whatever the truth about a left-hander's vulnerability to life, it should be remembered that not all alcoholics and accident victims are left-handed, and that being left-handed doesn't mean an individual will, by some inevitable force of fate, become an alcoholic, a candidate for suicide, or even particularly accident-prone.

Pigeonholes, after all, aren't made for people—they're for the birds.

The Advantages

Anecdotal testimony abounds as to the advantages of left-handedness. "It makes me a better basketball player." "Left-

A Left-Handed Job Applicant

handers are more creative and imaginative." "All the left-handers I know have a greater zest for life." "All the best architects are left-handed." "Left-handedness gives one an advantage in the arts." Unfortunately, medical science—so seemingly obsessed with what's *wrong* with left-handers—hasn't exerted much energy probing what's exceptional about them.

Over the years, a truly amazing assortment of characteristics have been anecdotally attributed to left-handed people.

Left-Handers Are:

more eccentric	more spiritual
less rigid	more psychic
more artistic	less conventional
better musicians	more innovative
more playful	more observant
better athletes	more sensual
less belligerent	better designers
less controlling	better mathematicians
more spontaneous	more intuitive
more absentminded	

Show this list to a majority of left-handers and ask whether most of it applies to them, and they'll say, "Of course."

The problem is, show the same list to a majority of right-handers and ask whether most of it applies to *them*—and the answer will *also* be, "Of course."

It all begins to sound like one of those Chinese-restaurant placemats ("Tell us the year you were born, and we'll tell you all about yourself"): specific enough to be flattering, but vague enough to suit anyone.

Some of the facts, then, about the very real advantages of being left-handed:

Left-handedness has been linked to exceptional mathematical and verbal abilities. Despite the reputation left-handers have for being slow to learn and verbally clumsy, studies

---

HAND-TO-HAND COMBAT

Perhaps one of the most unusual advantages of being left-handed was described by hockey player Wayne Cashman of the Boston Bruins. Cashman claimed that left-handedness gave him an advantage in the frequent fistfights that occurred on the ice. "The key to a hockey fight," he once remarked to an interviewer, "is the first punch. When you're a lefty and they're looking for the right, it helps."

---

have shown that among verbally precocious young people, there is a disproportionately high number of left-handers. In fact, one study at Johns Hopkins University found that of high school seniors scoring 630 or better on the verbal section of the SAT, more than 20 percent were left-handed—roughly twice the rate of left-handers in the general population. Left-handers are also overrepresented among the mathematically gifted. Left-handed males, in particular, tend to achieve higher than average scores on the mathematics section of the SAT.

Left-handers, on the whole, recover better from certain kinds of strokes and brain injuries. People who are left-handed have fewer problems with paralysis—and more quickly recover damaged functions such as speech—after a stroke or moderate injury. Some researchers have speculated that, by comparison with a right-hander's brain, the two hemispheres of a left-hander's brain function more equally, and one side is better prepared to take over if the other side is impaired.

Left-handedness gives some athletes a decided advantage in certain sports. About 50 percent of the players in the Baseball Hall of Fame are either left-handed or switch-hitters. And it's been estimated that nearly 40 percent of the top tennis pros are left-handed. Left-handers—either natural or "situational"—have an edge in both sports, as well as in boxing. (More about the left-handed sports advantage in chapters 8 and 9.) Meanwhile, because it has been tentatively linked to better underwater vision, left-handedness is also said to give swimmers and divers an advantage.

Left-handers have a better memory for music than right-handers. Studies have shown that left-handers have better pitch recall than right-handers, perhaps because the area of the brain that stores musical memory is typically located in the right hemisphere.

Left-handers have a better recovery rate than right-handers from severe hand injuries. Given that left-handers are regularly forced by necessity to use both of their hands in a primarily right-handed society, it should come as no surprise that they have an advantage over right-handers in adjusting to an injury to the dominant hand.

Left-handers are faster and more adept at typing and word processing. This is at least in part because left-handers are better at using both hands; but it's also because the keys most commonly struck—e, a, s, and t—are all on the left side of the keyboard.

Generally, left-handers can read backward (or backward *and* upside down) much better than right-handers. This unusual ability—though it has few practical advantages—may indicate a higher degree of certain kinds of mental flexibility among left-handed people.

If you can read this fluently, without straining too much, it's a good bet you're left-handed, since left-handers have a significant advantage reading backwards — or backwards and upside-down.

The Creativity Question

Are left-handers more creative than right-handers?

Are they more innovative and less bound by orthodox precepts and rigid models of problem solving?

The answer is: maybe.

In general, some studies *have* found a link—still nebulous and theoretical—between left-handedness and creativity. It may be correlated with the structure of the brain: with the larger than average corpus callosum enhancing "communication" between the two hemispheres, or with the way in which information, memory, and various skills are "processed" within some left-handers' brains.

It may also have something to do with the not insignificant fact that anytime you're not one of the majority, you have to become more creative. When you're not raised within the social parameters that most people grow up inside, you're sometimes free to look beyond them. For example, a left-handed child who must discover on his or her own how to write left-handedly in school (rather than with the carefully prescribed lessons developed for right-handed children) gets an early and potentially personality-shaping lesson in creative problem solving. (Unfortunately, that child may also get a lesson in aggravation and anxiety.)

A lot of questions remain to be answered on the entire issue. But, as Dr. Martin Luther King, Jr., once observed, "Human salvation lies in the hands of the creatively maladjusted."

Some Thoughts on Left-Handedness and Creativity

"Left-handed people, speaking in general, are creative. Now I've known some pretty dull people who were left-handed, but not as many as right-handed people."

—Actor Phil Grecian

"Right-handers are a bunch of chocolate soldiers. If you've seen one, you've seen 'em all."
—Neurosurgeon Dr. Joseph Bogan

"I'm sure it's not just chance that Pablo Picasso, Michelangelo, Leonardo da Vinci, and a long list of other artists have all been left-handed or ambidextrous. Their genius may well have had something to do with their left-handedness."
—Dr. Jeannine Herron, research psychologist in neuropsychiatry

"I don't think anyone is being kept from doing anything or is particularly helped by being left-handed. I don't think it's really an important issue."
—Art historian H. W. Janson

"Left-handed people show up in disproportionate numbers in the graphic arts. Among painters, Leonardo da Vinci, Raphael, Hans Holbein, Paul Klee, and Picasso were left-handed."
—Psychologist Dr. Stanley Coren

"Lefties are superior in creativity, tonal memory, spatial ability, originality, and elaboration of thinking. Social differentiation is of evolutionary benefit to any social group."
—Child psychologist Dr. Lauren Harris

"While lefties are only a small minority, you'd never know it from their long-standing creative impact. If it seems to you that an awful lot of lefties have made their mark in literature, music, and art, it's not your imagination."
—Free-lance writer Eileen Mazer

"It's not the kind of thing you pay a lot of attention to, but when you start looking at artists and noticing which hand they use, there are a lot of people in the art community who are left-handed."
—Barbara Haskell, curator, Whitney Museum of American Art

"Left-handed people tend to be more creative, more imaginative than right-handed people."
   —Dr. Brying Bryngelson, University of Minnesota

"Any group that includes Charlemagne, Rock Hudson, Paul McCartney, Leonardo da Vinci, Benjamin Franklin, Jack the Ripper, and the Boston Strangler must be select, if not elite."
   —Author James De Kay

7

Sinister Meanings: A Left-Hander's Guide to Language, Superstition, and Prejudice

left adj. From the Middle English, meaning "weak" or "useless."

sinister adj. Inauspicious, threatening, evil. From the Latin word *sinister*, meaning "on the left side."

A prejudice against the left hand—against the left side in general—exists in almost all languages and cultures.

In Israel, to have "two left hands" is to be insufferably clumsy.

In Japan, a "move to the left" is a job demotion.

In Spain, a "left-hander" is a malicious hoodlum or thief.

In France, "passing the weapon to the left" is an old slang expression for dying, comparable to our own "kicking the bucket."

The Russian language is full of such expressions. To have "gotten up on the left foot" is to have awakened in a foul mood. The "left side" of a piece of fabric or material is the wrong side. To do anything "on the left" means to do it sneakily. *Levak*—a "lefter"—is pejorative slang for a homosexual.

English also is riddled with idioms and slang expressions in which the connotation of "left" is clumsiness, duplicity, or outright evil:

To be out in left field is to be wildly mistaken, way off the mark.

A daughter of the left hand was, in Victorian times, a euphemism for a daughter born out of wedlock.

To have two left feet is to be clumsy; it's most frequently used to describe a poor dancer.

A left-handed compliment is an ambiguous put-down or sarcastic compliment, as in, "Well, isn't it nice to see you all dressed up for once?" or "Your hair actually looks very nice when you take the time to do something with it."

A left-handed oath is a promise you have no intention of keeping.

A left-handed toast is a toast drunk to someone's downfall (so named because it was once considered an insult to propose a toast to someone with the drink in your left hand).

To offer your left hand in friendship is to stab a friend in the back.

To see with the left eye is to have feeble vision or to see only what you want to see.

One can add to this list numerous other phrases with the same sense of reversal or negation: *left-handed* strokes of fortune (endless bad luck), a *left-handed* marriage (marrying beneath one's station), a *left-handed* conjecture (one that is vacuous or frivolous).

Other languages that have incorporated derogatory implications for the concept of *left* or *left-handedness* include Swahili, German, Italian, Serbo-Croatian, Arabic, Chinese, Turkish, and Portuguese. In fact, almost every known language betrays some bias against the left.

It's difficult to say exactly how all this prejudice against the left hand began. Many authorities believe it originated many hundreds of years ago (going back at least to Biblical times) with the fact that most people perform their toilet hygiene with the left hand. In many cultures the left hand is still vehemently viewed as the "unclean" hand. (The Arabs, for example, consider it tasteless and offensive to pass food or wine with the left hand.) Others point out that physical differences of any sort—left-handedness, unusual birthmarks, extra digits on a hand—have traditionally been feared by various societies and interpreted as marks of the Devil, or of inferiority. (When Henry VIII was trying to rid himself of Anne Boleyn, he contemplated using the fact that she had six fingers on her left hand as "proof" that she was an agent of the Devil—and it probably would have been an effective accusation.) As psychologist Dr. Robert Anthony has noted, "People concern themselves with being normal, rather than natural."

Whatever the origins, the left hand has long been laughed at, persecuted, discounted, and ridiculed.

In the English language, one of the earliest definitions for the word *left* was "weak" or "useless." That same connotation—and the related implication that everything to do with the *right* is somehow strong and skillful—survives today in countless words.

Awkward and **gawky** both come from a Middle English word, *awke*, meaning "from the left."

Gauche—meaning "tactless" or "lacking grace"—comes from the French word meaning "on the left" or "left-handed."

By contrast, **adroit** comes from the French word meaning "on the right." And **maladroit**—meaning "bungling" or "uncouth"—literally means "bad on the right."

Dexterous, meanwhile, comes from the Latin word *dexter*, meaning "the right hand," while **sinister** comes from the Latin word *sinister*, meaning "on the left side."

Even the word **ambidextrous** is subtly pejorative to left-handers. It literally means "having two right hands."

It should be noted that, separate from any connotation of ill fortune or clumsiness, the technical medical terms for handedness (*sinistrality* for left-handedness, *dextrality* for right-handedness) also come from those same Latin terms *sinister* and *dexter*. Among psychologists and researchers, left-handers are known as *sinistrals* and right-handers as *dextrals*.

Portsiders and Southpaws

In the face of all this, it's perhaps surprising that there are no derogatory terms for left-handed people in common usage in the English language. In fact, most of the terms—**lefties, left-handers, left-siders**—are straightforward. Add to these the not-unfriendly term **southpaws**, as well as **portsiders** (from the "port" side of a ship), **cat-handed** (popular in some parts of England), **pen-pushers** (from the fact that most left-handers have to push the pen across the paper when they write, instead of drag it as right-handers do), and the aforementioned **sinistrals**.

Two notable exceptions are the Australian slang term **molly-dukers** ("molly" meaning effeminate, and "dukers" referring to hands) and the British colloquialism **cack-handed** ("cack" being slang for excrement)—which brings us back to the odious notion of the "unclean" hand.

> *"The unwashen hand leads to blindness,*
> *the hand leads to deafness, the*
> *hand causes a polypus."*
>
> *—The Talmud*

Was Eve Left-Handed?

"Labels are devices for saving talkative persons the trouble of thinking."

—John Morley

Michelangelo portrayed Eve as having taken the forbidden fruit with her left hand, while the Flemish painter Jan van Eyck depicted her doing the same thing with her right. Whatever the truth of the matter, the Devil himself has traditionally been portrayed as left-handed or as lingering over the left side of his latest victim: hence the old superstition of tossing a pinch of salt over your left shoulder—"right into the Devil's face"—to ward off bad luck. And the left hand—the left *anything*—has, for centuries, been heaped with suggestions of sin, betrayal, and demon worship.

In the Middle Ages, it was said that saints sometimes revealed their piety very early in life by refusing to suckle their mother's left breast.

In the New Testament, Christ tells his disciples that on Judg-

LEFT-HANDED U.S. PLACE NAMES

Despite whatever prejudice has existed against the left hand (against the left *anything*), a scattering of places in the United States bear sinistral names, though in most instances "left" was used to refer to direction or geographical orientation:

Lefthand Bay, Alaska
Left Cape, Arkansas
Left Hand, West Virginia
Left Hand Spring, Oklahoma
Lefthand Creek, Colorado
Lefthand Luman Creek, Wyoming

The only one named after a person is Lefthand Creek, Colorado, named after a nineteenth-century fur trader, Andrew Sublette, who was left-handed.

ment Day, God will summon the faithful to his right side and the unsaved to his left: "Then shall he say also unto them on the left hand, Depart from me, ye cursed, into everlasting fire." Meanwhile, Judas has frequently been portrayed, in depictions of the Last Supper, as having been seated immediately to Christ's left.

The Devil is almost always depicted as holding his pitchfork in the left hand, while witches—his emissaries on earth—were long said to cause pain, disease, and injury with just a touch of the left hand.

Even today it is considered obligatory to offer or receive Communion, or to make the sign of the cross, with the right hand—not the left.

Leigh W. Rutledge and Richard Donley

A Miscellany of
Left-Handed Superstitions

A variety of cultures have long believed that if your right palm itches you're about to come into some money, but if your *left* palm itches you may soon be destitute. (The antidote, according to folklore, is to quickly rub your left palm on wood.)

In the nineteenth century, English thieves often refused to work with a left-handed safecracker or picklock, believing that, although such men were said to be quicker and more adept than their right-handed counterparts, they often brought bad luck and were invariably arrested.

From the time of ancient Rome up to the nineteenth century, it was regarded as an omen of extremely bad luck to accidentally put your right shoe on your left foot in the morning.

The left hind foot of a rabbit was once considered the luckiest kind of rabbit's foot to carry around. The English diarist Samuel Pepys even believed that his rabbit's foot had cured him of flatulence. "I am at a loss to know," he wrote, "whether it be my hare's foot which is my preservative against wind, for I never had a fit of collique since I wore it."

In certain parts of Africa, seeing a mongoose on the left side of the path when you are on your way to visit a sick friend means the friend will die. If you see a mongoose on the right side of the path, the friend will probably recover. (One commentator added, "If you see a mongoose in the center of the path and its lips are curled, your *own* health is in danger.")

According to an old Irish saying, dipping the left hand of a dead man in a pail of milk will cause the cream to form more quickly.

In several countries, the prohibition against getting out of bed on the left side is so strong it's recommended that, if you accidentally do it, you should walk backward, retracing your steps carefully, get back into the bed, and then get out again, this time on the right side. Otherwise your entire day will be beset by difficulties and bad luck.

The Romans, the ancient Egyptians, and even the Scots and

some Victorians believed that entering a house with the left foot called down bad luck and evil forces on the inhabitants. Some wealthy Romans went so far as to employ doormen whose sole duty was to make certain all guests entered the house with the right foot first.

The seventeenth-century Spanish poet Francisco de Quevedo warned, " 'Tis not safe trusting a left-handed man with money."

Leigh W. Rutledge and Richard Donley

The Wisdom of the Zunis

Admittedly, there are some superstitions that are well disposed to the left hand. Among the Zuni Indians, for example, the left side of the body represents wisdom and contemplation, while the right side symbolizes impulsiveness and a desire for action. The Zunis believe that of the two hands, the left is the older and the wiser.

Prejudice in the Schoolroom

In the early 1900s, American writer and educator A. N. Palmer held symposiums across the country explaining that left-handed children should be forced to write with their right hands, whether they liked it or not. His rationale was simple: it's a right-handed world, and young people must be taught the value of conformity.

Until a few decades ago, left-handed schoolchildren were an easy target for parents and teachers—especially teachers, most of whom insisted that their left-handed pupils learn to write with their right hands. The methods employed were often extreme: tying the left hand to the desk so the student couldn't use it, whacking the left hand with a ruler to "condition" the student to write "'properly," loudly berating or humiliating a child for left-handedness in front of the other students. The USSR, China, Germany, and many of the Iron Curtain countries were particularly unforgiving in this respect: writing with the left hand was forbidden altogether. Left-handed Soviet émigrés often have unusual stories of their treatment at school: heavy, cumbersome weights tied to their left hands (the idea was to weigh it down so it couldn't be used, but as one Ukrainian woman later noted with irony, "All it did was make my left hand stronger"), having their left arms tied behind their backs twenty-four hours a day, even having scalding water poured on their left hands.

In the United States, things were scarcely better, though it

LEFTISTS VS. RIGHT-WINGERS

The political terms "left-wing" and "right-wing" ("left" for liberals, "right" for conservatives) didn't arise from any bias toward the left hand or any superstitions about the left side being weak or emotional. According to Thomas Carlyle in his monumental *The French Revolution*, the terms evolved during the pivotal French Assembly of 1789, when it became customary for the radicals and revolutionaries to sit together to the left of the presiding officer, while the more conservative aristocrats sat to the right. Hence, those who favored sweeping social reforms were of the "left wing" of the Assembly, while those who fought to maintain the status quo were of the "right wing."

always depended on the individual teacher. And even when the teacher was more enlightened and didn't forbid the use of the left hand in penmanship, southpaws were still often left to their own devices trying to figure out *how* to write left-handedly. Few teachers, for example, simply told them to try tilting the paper thirty degrees to the right, just as right-handers tilt the paper thirty degrees to the left.

Sadly, the same prejudices often extended to home. In fact, during the first half of the twentieth century, some parents exhibited an inexplicable fanaticism on the subject, and seemed to equate left-handedness with deformity or sickness. "What's *wrong* with my daughter?" a mother would ask the doctor. "She's left-handed." Or a left-handed child might be met with a disparaging, "You can't possibly be left-handed. There *are* no left-handers in our family!" If such treatment was persistent and the parent was "successful" in breaking the child's "obstinacy," the result was sometimes dyslexia, stuttering, feelings of inferiority, and an inability to tell left from right.

All of which just goes to show that of all superstitions, a mania for conformity is probably the worst.

8

Baseball: The Great Left-Handed Pastime

Are left-handers overrepresented in professional baseball? The statistics would certainly seem to indicate so. Of 142,821 "at bats" in major-league play in 1989, 41 percent were by left-handed batters; 32 percent were against left-handed pitchers. The rules of the game, the configuration of certain ballparks, even the laws of physics—all, in one way or another, favor left-handed play at times. In fact, through the years, a number of otherwise right-handed individuals—Yogi Berra, Carl Yastrzemski, and Maury Wills, among others—have chosen to play at least some part of the game left-handedly in order to improve their chances for victory.

Left-handed baseball players can be divided into two categories: those who are naturally left-handed, and those (like Berra and Yastrzemski) who are merely "situational." It's difficult to tell exactly how many natural left-handers have played the game professionally. However, among Baseball Hall of Famers, 22 percent of the pitchers and 19 percent of the other players have been left-handed throwers. This is significant because the way a player throws the ball is probably more indicative of his actual hand preference than is the way he wields a bat. (Some researchers speculate that, in general, throwing may be an even more revealing indication of hand preference than writing.) It would appear that natural left-handers are about twice as prevalent in the ballpark as they are in the general population. There's

HOW SINISTER ARE THE MEMBERS OF BASEBALL'S HALL OF FAME?

Positions	Total Hall of Famers	Left-handers Throwers	Batters	Switch- Hitters
First basemen	15	8	9	0
Second basemen	13	0	5	2
Shortstops	16	0	3	1
Third basemen	7	0	2	0
Left fielders	18	6	11	0
Center fielders	14	2	8	2
Right fielders	20	6	11	1
Catchers	11	0	3	0
Total	114	22	52	6
Percentage of the Total	100	19	46	5
Pitchers	49	11	7	7
Percentage of the Total	100	22	14	14

Source: The National Baseball Hall of Fame and Museum, Inc.

little doubt that some of the traits frequently ascribed to left-handers—a keen sense of spatial relationship, a tendency toward ambidexterity—would have certain advantages in the game. Those traits, in combination with the logistical benefits that left-handed play sometimes provides, may give some players a powerful edge.

How many professional ballplayers are "situational" left-handers? Estimating deductively from the statistics, the figure is about 20 percent.

Left-Handers Are Strikingly Good Batters

Compared to the right-hander, the left-handed batter has a better chance of:

Keeping his eye on the ball. A right-handed batter has to turn his head farther to track a ball thrown by a right-handed pitcher, because it's thrown from the same side of the mound that he's standing on. By contrast, because a left-handed batter stands on the first-base side of home plate, he doesn't have to turn his head as far to follow the trajectory of a right-handed pitch.

Hitting the ball. Because balls that curve toward the batter are easier to hit than those that curve away from him, a left-handed batter has a distinct advantage when facing a right-handed pitcher (which happens about 70 percent of the time). A pitch tends to curve away from the side from which it is thrown—which means that a right-handed pitch curves *toward* a left-handed batter. (Of course, the converse is also true: right-handed batters are more successful against left-handed pitchers.)

Getting on base. Upon completing his swing, the left-hander is facing first base and his body momentum is in that direction. By contrast, a right-hander is headed toward third base on completion of his swing, and must change his body momentum before starting to first. Also, a left-handed batter stands on the right side of home plate, slightly shortening the distance between him and first base.

Hitting home runs. Many baseball stadiums have shallow right outfields. This benefits left-handed batters, since they tend to hit the ball in that direction. In fact, it was the shallow right

"Right-handers are steadier than left-handers. They steady an infield. The southpaws are usually temperamental and easily rattled. They are also inclined to fancy 'show off' playing, such as overdoing the one-hand catch."
—Sports columnist E. V. Durling,
San Francisco Examiner, 1956

outfield of Yankee Stadium that helped enhance the careers and home run tallies of such left-handed sluggers as Babe Ruth and Lou Gehrig.

Powerful Pitching Southpaws

"They throw crooked, they walk crooked and they think crooked. They even wear their clothes crooked. You have to figure they're a little crazy."

—Al Schacht on left-handed pitchers

One of the only concrete advantages that a left-handed pitcher enjoys is an ability to keep a tighter rein on first base. (A right-handed pitcher has to look over his shoulder to see first; a left-handed pitcher is already facing it during his stretch motion.) Left-handed pitchers also have the advantage of handicapping left-handed batters (for roughly the same reasons that left-handed batters have an advantage over right-handed pitchers). Beyond that, there probably aren't enough tangible reasons to explain why so many pitchers are left-handed. The benefits of left-handed pitching are poorly understood. Southpaw pitchers may have a slight (and very tenuous) psychological advantage against certain players, since for years they've had the reputation of being "weird" and "crazy"; in other words, some batters find them intimidating.

Baseball pitchers are, by the way, the only group of people in

> Brooks Robinson, the great Oriole third baseman, batted and threw right-handed, but signed autographs with his left hand.
>
> Both Babe Ruth and Stan Musial batted and threw with their left hands, but signed autographs with their right.

the world routinely described according to their hand preference: "Southpaw Steve Avery's two 1–0 victories got him the Most Valuable Player Award . . ." "Dodger left-hander Fernando Valenzuela . . ." "Southpaw legend Sandy Koufax . . ."

Disadvantages for Left-Handed Players

There are some positions in which left-handed players face a disadvantage in the ballpark.

Left-handers are seldom found at second or third base, or at a shortstop position, because they have to pivot to throw to first base.

There hasn't been a regular left-handed catcher in the major leagues for years, although two left-handers—Benny De Stefano and Mike Squires—did catch in several games in the 1980s. Left-handed catchers are considered to be at a disadvantage because a right-handed batter obstructs their line of fire to second.

There are a few southpaw left fielders; but they have to turn their bodies to throw to second base if they field the ball between themselves and the foul line.

On the other hand, first base is traditionally a haven for southpaws. In fact, more than half the Hall of Fame first basemen were left-handed. They have an edge in fielding grounders and bunts, and in throwing to second.

Three Legends

Tyrus Raymond "Ty" Cobb (1886–1961)
Batted left-handed, threw right-handed

As a young man, Cobb accidentally shot himself in the left shoulder with a .22 rifle. The slug remained in him for the rest of his life, but it didn't stop him from batting—left-handedly— 4,191 hits (second only to Pete Rose's 4,256) or from scoring 2,245 runs (still a major-league record). No player has ever bested Cobb's .367 lifetime batting average. In fact, Cobb created or tied more major-league records than any other player during his years with the Detroit Tigers. He's been called a Pete Rose with better hitting, slicker base running, and smarter accountants. Cobb was the first millionaire athlete, having amassed a fortune in stock in General Motors and Coca-Cola.

His benign nickname, "the Georgia Peach," hardly seemed to fit a man who was perhaps the fiercest competitor and most disliked player in the sport. Long on ambition and short on humor, he was arrested several times for getting into fights both in and out of the ballpark. On more than one occasion, he jumped into the stands to physically assault a heckling spectator. (He was suspended for ten days in 1912 after beating one spectator unconscious.) And it was said he liked to sharpen his spikes before a game so that when he slid feet-first into a base, he could inflict as much damage as possible on the defending baseman.

His greatness came not so much from raw power or natural talent as from a hardened determination and steely intelligence. He was a master strategist who stayed one step ahead of the competition, both as a batsman and as a base runner. He set numerous records for stealing bases and still holds the record for stealing home plate—thirty-five times. (He sometimes stole second base, then proceeded to third as the throw came in behind him.)

Cobb dominated the sport of baseball from the turn of the century until shortly after World War I. Then the game changed forever. A "livelier" ball (one that could be hit out of the ballpark with some regularity) was introduced, and an even more monumental figure came onto the scene. The Babe Ruth era had dawned.

George Herman "Babe" Ruth (1895–1948)
Batted left-handed, threw left-handed

More than half a century after hitting his last home run (not for the Yankees, but for the Boston Braves) on May 25, 1935, Ruth is still the most famous and beloved sports figure of all time. He was well known for his various foibles—smoking, drinking, and occasional womanizing—and his training was lax at best; but the weaknesses never overshadowed the achievements of this 6′2″, 200-pound giant.

George Herman Ruth was born in Baltimore, and by the time he was seven he was already so unruly his parents sent him to a Catholic boys' school, where the monks first taught him to play ball. Although he wrote right-handed, he pitched and batted left-handed. Despite a few minor handicaps—he had to use a right-handed catcher's mitt because no left-handed mitts were available—he was obviously a prodigious talent, and by the age of nineteen he was already playing professionally.

Although he started out as a pitcher—probably the best left-handed pitcher of the time—it soon became obvious that he was even more valuable as a hitter. His powerful left-handed swing fostered a string of memorable nicknames:

> "Sultan of Swat"
> "Rajah of Rap"
> "Colossus of Clout"
> "Caliph of Clout"
> "Maharajah of Mash"
> "Behemoth of Bust"
> "Wazir of Wham"

Year by year, his fame and his salary grew. He played ball for the Yankees from 1920 to 1934, and Yankee Stadium became known as "the House That Ruth Built." In 1930, when he de-

Some of the best baseball players—like Mickey Mantle—have been switch-hitters. They generally bat "opposite" the pitcher. If the pitcher is a right-hander, they bat left-handed; if the pitcher is a southpaw, they bat right-handed. But what happens if a switch-hitter faces one of those rare hurlers who can pitch with either hand?

In 1976, ambidextrous pitcher Audrey Scruggs of the Kingsport, Tennessee, Braves paired off against switch-hitter Dan Spain of the Elizabethton, Tennessee, Twins. *Sports Illustrated* vividly described the resulting standoff: "When switch pitcher Scruggs faced switch hitter Dan Spain . . . there was a three-minute minuet during which Scruggs kept changing hands and Spain kept jumping back and forth across the plate, each seeking a tactical advantage. The umpire finally ordered Spain to commit himself, and he chose to bat right-handed. Scruggs, throwing rightly, retired him on an infield grounder."

manded—and got—an unprecedented $80,000 contract, someone indignantly observed that he was making more money than President Hoover. "I had a better year," Ruth replied.

Not only could he hit the ball farther than anyone else (sometimes he swung so hard he almost fell over when he missed), but he did it with stunning frequency. Even though Roger Maris and Hank Aaron eventually bested his single-season and lifetime home run records, no one has ever come close to his home run average: he hit a homer once out of every 11.8 times at bat—714 home runs in all. Leading the Yankees to seven pennant wins and four World Series triumphs, he almost seemed invincible, but he made his share of blunders: he was, for instance, the only major-league ballplayer ever to lose a World Series by being tagged out while stealing a base.

He was uncouth and at times ill-mannered—he sometimes hit umpires and occasionally chased a disrespectful fan—but to his adoring followers, that only contributed to the Babe Ruth mystique. He basked in the adulation of his admirers, but always gave back what he received. Never ashamed of his own less than glamorous origins, he donated much of his time and money to helping underprivileged youngsters, and rarely refused a request to visit the sickbed of a dying child. It was amazing what a visit from the Babe could do for a child's morale.

Henry Louis "Lou" Gehrig (1903–1941)
Batted left-handed, threw left-handed

To this day, Gehrig remains one of the most compelling figures in baseball, not only because of his achievements (or because of his tragic death), but because he cut such an unlikely figure in the sport he excelled at. An alumnus of Columbia University, he was a quiet, thoughtful man, so modest and so openly devoted to his mother that sportswriters hardly knew how to classify him, especially compared to the rough-hewn earthiness of Babe Ruth or the abrasive "winning is everything" arrogance of Ty Cobb.

Nicknamed "the Iron Horse" and "the Pride of the Yankees," Gehrig achieved one of the most extraordinary records in baseball history: between 1925 and 1939, he played 2,130 consecutive games, often despite various physical ailments (in 1934, he had to be carried off the field after a severe attack of lumbago, a problem he struggled with for much of his career). His other achievements, one after the other, contributed to the legend:

- In 1932, he hit four consecutive home runs in one game.

- During seven seasons, he had 150 or more RBIs, including 184 in 1931.

- In 1934, and again in 1936, he hit 49 home runs.

- In 34 games in 7 World Series, he hit 10 home runs, drove in 35 runs, and batted .361

Gehrig finished his career with 1,990 RBIs, 493 home runs, and a .340 batting average.

It was in 1939, at the age of thirty-five, that he felt compelled to pull himself out of the game. For a long time, he'd been having difficulties with a wide variety of perplexing symptoms:

muscles that refused to work right, chronic fatigue, vision problems. A series of tests at the Mayo Clinic brought the verdict:
he had amyotrophic lateral sclerosis, a mysterious and usually
fatal syndrome in which the body's muscles relentlessly atrophy.
"Today I consider myself the luckiest man on the face of the
earth," he told tens of thousands of fans assembled at Yankee
Stadium for Lou Gehrig Day on July 14, 1939.

Two years later, he was dead, and the illness that killed him
(and which later struck such notables as David Niven, Rory Fos-
ter, and Stephen Hawking) became universally known as Lou
Gehrig's disease.

Left-Handed Larceny:
Successful Base Stealers

Maury Wills (b. 1932)

As a shortstop with various farm clubs for seven years, the
right-handed Wills had little prospect of ever playing major-
league baseball—until his manager suggested he bat left-handed
against right-handed pitchers. Wills was, if nothing else, determined: he made this unusual midcareer conversion with barely
a hitch. He still wasn't a power hitter, but he was able to bunt
and bounce the ball around the infield and get safely to first
often enough to do what he was really good at—stealing bases.

In 1960, a year after he finally joined the Dodgers, he stole
fifty bases—the most recorded in the National League since
1923.

In 1962, he stole 104 bases, besting Ty Cobb's old single-
season record of 96.

Wills's exploits on the diamond thrilled fans and inspired other
players (most notably, Lou Brock and Rickey Henderson). By
bringing back the forgotten art of base stealing, the artful Dodger
helped reenergize the game.

Lou Brock (b. 1939)

"Everything moves wrong," teammate Bob Gibson once said of Lou Brock's style on the dance floor; "you never saw any-body so clumsy." Graceless or not, Brock had more than 3,000 hits playing for the Cardinals between 1961 and 1979. However, his greatest accomplishment was breaking Ty Cobb's long-standing career stolen-base record. A total of 938 stolen bases wasn't bad for a left-handed outfielder who couldn't dance.

Rickey Henderson (b. 1957)

On May 1, 1991, Rickey Henderson stole his 939th base, breaking Lou Brock's old career record. "Lou Brock was a great base stealer," Henderson announced to his fans, "but today I am the greatest of all time." Henderson—who is one of those rare players who throws with the left hand but bats right-handed—perfected an unusual style: stealing bases by lunging headfirst at the sack.

Remarkable Left-Handed
Home Run Achievements

"Duke" Snider (b. 1926)

Snider's father, a semipro ballplayer, taught him to bat left-handed because "Most major-league parks are built for left-handed hitters." The lesson paid off handsomely: the naturally right-handed Snider became a powerful left-handed home run slugger for the Brooklyn Dodgers.

In the 1952 World Series, he hit four home runs, matching feats by Lou Gehrig and Babe Ruth.

Three years later, during the 1955 World Series, he hit four home runs again—and the Dodgers finally beat the Yankees.

Unfortunately for Snider, the Dodgers moved to Los Angeles in 1958. Their new home was a converted football stadium with a practically limitless right field, and the Duke's home run hitting was sharply curtailed. He ended his career in 1962 with 407 home runs to his credit.

Mel Ott (1909–1958)

When Ott stood at the plate, he looked like any other left-handed batter—until he swung. When the pitcher discharged the ball, Ott lifted his right leg high, then slammed it back to the ground as the ball met the bat. In this foot-stamping fashion, he hit 511 home runs for the New York Giants between 1926 and 1947.

Ted Williams (b. 1918)

Ted Williams might have hit more home runs than Babe Ruth—if it hadn't been for war. He wound up losing five prime ball-playing years to military service, first during World War II, then during the Korean War. As it was, Williams hit 521 home runs and had a lifetime batting average of .344 in a career spanning two decades with the Boston Red Sox. His wrist action was so fast—and so precise—that he usually waited until the very last moment to swing at a pitch. Widely regarded as the greatest hitter of his time, Williams was the last major-league player to bat over .400. His peak was .406 in 1941.

Reggie Jackson (b. 1946)

Jackson struck out more times than any other player in major-league history (2,597 times, to be exact), but he more than made up for it with his 563 home runs. In twenty-one seasons, "Mr. October" was on eleven division-winning teams and participated in five World Series. His greatest triumph came in the 1977 World Series, when he powered the Yankees to victory over the Dodgers—by hitting a record-breaking five home runs, including three in one game.

Willie McCovey (b. 1938)

In 1968, and again in 1969, McCovey led the National League in RBIs, home runs, and slugging percentage. He hit a total of 521 home runs during his career.

Don Mattingly (b. 1961)

Though naturally ambidextrous, Mattingly made an early choice to bat and throw exclusively with his left hand, in order to better his chances of making it into the major leagues. The strategy worked. He batted .343 in 1983 and .352 in 1986, and he has become one of the most powerful home run sluggers in the major leagues: in 1987, he set a new major-league record by hitting six grand slams. He is considered one of the game's best first basemen. He is also the last major-league left-hander to have played second and third base.

Darryl Strawberry (b. 1962)

"The Straw Man" hit one of his home runs right into the top hat that sits in the Mets' deep center field: the ball wound up jamming the machinery that lifts the big apple out of the hat whenever the team scores a homer. The celebrated outfielder hit 39 home runs for the New York Mets in 1988, and 37 more (along with 108 RBIs) in 1990. In 1991, he was lured back to his native Los Angeles when the Dodgers offered him a five-year, $20-million contract.

Left-Handed Heavy Hitters

Rod Carew (b. 1945)

"Trying to sneak a pitch past him," said Catfish Hunter, "is like trying to sneak the sunrise past a rooster." During his eighteen-year career with the Minnesota Twins, Carew had 3,053 hits and was the American League batting champion seven times. His lifetime batting average was .328, with fifteen consecutive seasons over .300, including a high of .388 in 1977.

George Brett (b. 1953)

Between 1975 and 1988, Brett batted over .300 ten times, and his .390 average for 1980 remains the highest in the major leagues since Ted Williams batted .406 in 1941. After he led the Royals to a World Series victory in 1985, "Brett for President" bumper stickers were seen all over Kansas City.

Willie Keeler (1872–1923)

Left-hander "Wee" Willie Keeler may have looked, according to his teammates, more like a batboy than one of the players; but his strategy ("I hit 'em where they ain't") gave him a .345 career batting average. Between 1892 and 1910, he played for the Dodgers, the Giants, and the Orioles.

George Sisler (1893–1973)

Like Babe Ruth, Sisler started out as a left-handed pitcher (for the St. Louis Browns), but he was eventually moved to first base because of his prowess at bat. His fielding was superb, his hitting phenomenal. In 1920, he batted .407 and collected 257 hits— still a major-league record. In 1922, his batting average was an astonishing .420, and he hit safely in 41 consecutive games—an American League record that wasn't broken until Joe DiMaggio's sensational hitting streak in the summer of 1941.

Stan Musial (b. 1920)

"Stan the Man" started playing ball for the St. Louis Cardinals in 1941; it was an alliance that lasted for twenty-two years. His record speaks for itself: seven league batting titles, voted Most Valuable Player three times, a lifetime batting average of .331 on 3,630 hits. When Musial was moved to left field—an unusual position for a left-hander—the Cardinals manager cheerfully defended the action: "When a boy has baseball instinct like that Musial, he can make the plays upside down."

Bill Terry (1896–1989)

The celebrated New York Giants first baseman was a brilliant line drive hitter. He was the last National League player to bat over .400: his average in 1930 was .401.

Leon "Goose" Goslin (1900–1971)

The Washington Senators may have been the worst team in the league ("First in war, first in peace, last in the American League"), but that didn't stop their star outfielder, Leon Goslin, from batting in 100 or more runs in each of eleven seasons. Goslin's regular play, however, was nothing compared to his performance in World Series competition. In the 1924 Series, he had six consecutive hits (a record), and he belted in three home runs each in both the '24 and '25 Series. After the 1933 season, he was traded to Detroit, where his hitting propelled the team to pennant victories in 1934 and 1935. His ninth-inning single in the sixth game of the '35 Series gave Detroit the championship.

Glory on the Mound:
A Gallery of Southpaw Pitchers

Eddie Plank (1875–1926)

Plank drove batters to distraction with his strange behavior on the mound: talking to the ball and sometimes fussing for several minutes with his uniform. Apparently the ball was listening—he was the first pitcher of the modern baseball era to win 300 games.

"Lefty" Grove (1900–1975)

Considered by some experts to be the greatest baseball pitcher of all time, Grove was a fastball phenomenon for the Philadelphia Athletics during the 1920s and 1930s. He won 31 and lost 4 in 1931, and ended his career with 300 wins against only 141 losses. Renowned for his tantrums after a loss, he still had enough self-possession to make sure he always punched a locker with his right hand, thereby protecting his left.

Carl Hubbell (1903–1988)

The master of the screwball (and known affectionately to his teammates as "the Meal Ticket"), Hubbell pitched for the New York Giants from 1928 to 1943 and established a 253–154 career record. However, he regularly discharged the ball with such a powerful clockwise snap of the wrist that eventually his entire left arm was disfigured. His left hand became permanently twisted with the palm facing out.

George "Rube" Waddell (1876–1914)

Waddell, who pitched for the Philadelphia Athletics before World War I, is rated by some authorities as the fastest left-handed pitcher of all time. However, he never drew a regular salary for his work: instead, he'd go to the manager for five or ten dollars whenever he needed it. His frequently odd behavior (obsessed with firemen, he'd sometimes forgo a game to watch

LEFT-HANDED PITCHERS

Steve Avery	Mark Langston
Vida Blue	Charlie Leibrandt
Steve Carlton	Sparky Lyle
Dave Dravecky	Tug McGraw
Chuck Finley	Hal Newhouser
Whitey Ford	Francis Joseph "Lefty" O'Doul
Tommy Glavine	Mel Parnell
Vernon "Lefty" Gomez	Billy Pierce
"Lefty" Grove	Eddie Plank
Ron Guidry	Dave Righetti
Willie Hernandez	John Smiley
Joe Hesketh	Warren Spahn
Carl Hubbell	Mike Stanton
Bruce Hurst	John Tudor
Danny Jackson	George "Lefty" Tyler
Tommy John	Fernando Valenzuela
Randy Jones	Frank Viola
Jim Kaat	George "Rube" Waddell
Sandy Koufax	Mitch Williams

them put out fires; other times, he showed up for a game drunk) contributed to the notion that all left-handed pitchers are flaky and crazy.

Johnny Vander Meer (b. 1914)

In 1938, Vander Meer became the only pitcher in major-league history to throw back-to-back no-hitters.

Warren Spahn (b. 1921)

Spahn was known for consistency and control. "Home plate is seventeen inches wide," he once told an interviewer, "but I ignore the middle twelve inches . . . I pitch to the two-and-a-half inches on each side." His accuracy was surpassed only by his durability: as a hurler for the Boston (later the Milwaukee)

Braves from 1946 to 1963, he racked up an astonishing 363 wins. And his major-league career didn't even begin until after World War II, when he was twenty-six years old.

Ron Guidry (b. 1950)

Guidry was instrumental in securing World Series victories for the Yankees in 1977 and 1978. In 1978, he had a phenomenal 25–3 season and won the Cy Young Award. He was still going strong in 1985, when he pitched a 22–6 season. He retired three years later. His ninety-mile-per-hour fastball was nicknamed "Louisiana Lightning."

Vida Blue (b. 1949)

Blue has been credited with single-handedly reviving a national interest in baseball in the early 1970s. During his first full year pitching for the Oakland A's in 1971, home game attendance *quadrupled* from the previous year. His stylish delivery (he added an unusual snap of the wrist as the ball left his hand), his good looks, and his stunning accuracy (his first season he was 24–8) all contributed to his tremendous appeal. He turned down a $2,000 offer from A's manager Charlie Finley to have his name legally changed to "True Blue."

Tommy John (b. 1943)

Nicknamed "Baseball's Bionic Man," John severely injured his elbow while pitching for the Dodgers in 1974 and later underwent one of the world's first ligament transplants to have it repaired. The procedure involved taking a tendon from the right forearm and transplanting it to the left elbow; hence the joke that he was baseball's first "right-handed southpaw." The operation was successful, and he returned to the mound to win twenty games in 1977. He retired in 1986.

Fernando Valenzuela (b. 1960)

In 1981, after pitching eight shutouts and leading the Dodgers to a world championship, Valenzuela became an international

celebrity. In his native Mexico, he was acclaimed as *Zurdo*—"the Left-hander." His famous screwball was nicknamed "Fernando's Fadeaway."

Billy Pierce (b. 1927)

Pierce's delivery was so smooth and precise when he pitched for the Chicago White Sox in the 1950s that one sportswriter dubbed him "the epitome of the stylish lefty."

Vernon "Lefty" Gomez (1908–1989)

Gomez compiled an enviable 189–102 record pitching for the Yankees from 1930 to 1942. However, he was at least as famous for his humor and antics. He acquired the nickname

---

LEFT-HANDED BATTERS
(BUT THEY THREW RIGHT-HANDED)

Yogi Berra	Bill Dickey
Wade Boggs	"Shoeless" Joe Jackson
George Brett	Joe Morgan
Rod Carew	Ted Williams
Ty Cobb	Carl Yastrzemski
Eddie Collins	

"Goofy" after publicly announcing his latest "invention"—a revolving goldfish bowl that saved its occupants the necessity of swimming. He liked to tell fans that even his pet Chihuahua was left-handed. The proof, according to Gomez: "When the dog goes to the fireplug, he raises his left leg."

Sandy Koufax (b. 1935)

When he was thirty-six, Koufax became the youngest player ever elected to the Baseball Hall of Fame. He was nicknamed "the Man with the Golden Arm." Between 1962 and 1966 (the year of his retirement), his win-loss record for the Dodgers was 14–7, 25–5, 19–5, 26–8, and 27–9. He averaged more than one strikeout per inning over the course of his career, and won the Cy Young Award three times. He retired from the game after doctors warned him he'd eventually lose the use of his left arm if he continued pitching.

"Whitey" Ford (b. 1926)

Widely regarded as the best Yankee pitcher (he was nicknamed the team's "Chairman of the Board"), Ford had a career record of 236–106 and helped catapult the team to eleven pennant victories in the 1950s and 1960s. He received the Cy Young Award in 1961.

LEFT-HANDED BATTERS WHO
ALSO *THREW* LEFT-HANDED

Barry Bonds	Stan Musial
Lou Brock	Babe Ruth
Sam Crawford	George Sisler
Lou Gehrig	Tris Speaker
Keith Hernandez	Darryl Strawberry
Reggie Jackson	Bill Terry
Don Mattingly	Paul Waner
Willie McCovey	

Dave Dravecky (b. 1956)

Dravecky worked his way up from the minor leagues to eventually become a starter for the San Diego Padres. In 1987, he was traded to the Giants and that same year, as he was preparing for playoffs against the St. Louis Cardinals, he suddenly noticed a small, seemingly insignificant bump on his left shoulder. He ignored it, but over the next few months it grew larger. It turned out to be a cancerous tumor.

Shortly after they removed the growth, doctors told him he had "zero chance" of ever pitching again. He refused to give in. "I have a passion for the game, for competition, for winning," he once told an interviewer. Despite the fact that almost half the muscle tissue in his throwing arm had been removed along with the tumor, he embarked on a ten-month program of intensive rehabilitation. In August 1989, with the cancer seemingly in remission and his pitching arm back in shape, Dravecky returned to the mound. It was, he later recalled, "the greatest moment" of his career. Giants fans gave him a standing ovation, and he proceeded to pitch, for seven innings, a nearly perfect one-hit game against the Cincinnati Reds.

It was in Montreal five days later that one of the most memorable comebacks in baseball history came to an abrupt and agonizing end. During the sixth inning of the game, Dravecky threw a wild pitch—and collapsed in agony on the mound. He had broken his shoulder: the sound of the bone snapping had been so loud the catcher could hear it. A new diagnosis of cancer followed a short time later, and there were new rounds of surgery, as well as radiation therapy; but finally the entire left arm and shoulder had to be amputated. The cancer, thankfully, hadn't spread.

Dravecky gives much of the credit for his eventual recovery to his devoted wife and children. In great demand as a public speaker now, he travels around the country describing his ordeal and trying, as he says, "to give others hope."

It isn't for lack of skill or determination that he won't be remembered as one of baseball's greatest pitchers. It *is* likely, however, that he'll be remembered as one of the bravest.

Two in the Dugout

Tommy Lasorda (b. 1927)

The feisty and highly successful left-handed manager of the Los Angeles Dodgers piloted the team to world championships in 1981 and 1988. In his sixties, Lasorda still swims 100 laps at a time. He says he's trying to work up to 150.

Casey Stengel (1891–1975)

"I was not successful as a ballplayer, as it was a game of skill."
> *—Left-hander Casey Stengel*

From 1949 to 1960, Stengel led the New York Yankees to ten pennant victories and seven world championships. Never one to walk away from a challenge, he became the first manager of the newly formed New York Mets in 1962, when he was seventy-one. The Mets soon established themselves as so hopelessly bad that everyone loved them. ("Can't anyone here play this game?" Stengel yelled to his players during one game.) The team, and Stengel, provided fodder for good-natured jokes across the country, becoming, among other things, a staple of

The Tonight Show's opening monologue for several years running. Said Jimmy Breslin, "This is a team for the cabdriver who gets held up in traffic and the guy who loses out on a promotion because he didn't maneuver himself to lunch with the boss enough."

Stengel himself had originally intended to become a dentist. However, when he started wielding dental tools left-handedly at school, one of his professors cried out in horror, "You're a left-hander, a left-hander!" Stengel soon abandoned the pursuit of dentistry in favor of baseball. He later joked, "I was a left-handed dentist who made people cry." Still, he was content to be a southpaw. "Left-handers," he often said, "have more enthusiasm for life."

His antics in the ballpark were legendary. Once he furtively captured a bird in the dugout and quickly stuck it under his cap: later, in a dispute with an umpire, he doffed his cap in the umpire's direction and the bird flew out. The fans were delighted. His Gracie Allen logic produced several memorable gems. "The team," he once said of the Mets, "has come along slow, but fast." On another occasion he announced, "There comes a time in every man's life—and I've had many of them."

9

Left-Handers in Other Sports

Basketball

As in many other sports, the element of surprise contributes to the left-hander's slight edge in basketball. Left-handed players are considered tough to defend against, because they usually handle the ball with the "wrong" hand (at least from the standpoint of right-handed opponents). But the advantage may not be as great as supposed, since their left side is covered by the defender's usually stronger right hand. The biggest advantage for left-handers in basketball probably occurs on defense, where they are sometimes in a better position to block a right-hander's shot. Hand preference is not much of a factor in the sport: the NBA doesn't even keep records of who is left- and right-handed. Most professionals, in fact, are quite adept at dribbling, passing, and shooting with either hand.

Levsha ("Lefty")

Left-hander Iuliana Semenova of the former USSR is both the tallest (almost 7'2") and heaviest (284 pounds) female Olympic gold medalist of all time. She won gold medals in women's basketball in the 1976 and 1980 summer games.

Larry Bird

Some Left-Handed Basketball Greats

Bill Russell
Bill Walton
Bob Lanier
Guy Rodgers
Lenny Wilkins
Nate Archibald
Larry Bird
Dave Cowens

Adrian Dantley
Digger Phelps
Walter Berry
Ron Kellogg
Mark Eaton
Wayman Tisdale
Charles "Lefty" Driesell
Dick Motta

Billiards

Left-hander Steve Mizerak, Jr., was the U.S. Open Pool champion four times during the 1970s. He won the 1976 World Open by shooting, left-handed, a perfect 150-ball run—a feat that his opponent, Rusty Miller, likened to "swimming the English Channel underwater." Mizerak's talent didn't make him rich (tournament stakes were quite modest). Nor did his sharpshooting make him famous—until he appeared in a series of commercials for Miller Lite beer doing some of the most intriguing trick shots ever recorded on camera.

Bowling

During a 1971 Professional Bowlers Association of America tournament in San Jose, California, all sixteen bowlers who survived to the finals were left-handed. Right-handed bowlers threatened to boycott future PBA events: they claimed that the lack of wear on the left side of most bowling lanes gave an unfair advantage to left-handed bowlers. In response, the PBA instituted a lane maintenance program designed to make all lanes "hand neutral" before each tournament. Even so, some bowling alleys are still regarded as favoring one hand over the other.

Left-handed bowling champion Patty Costello—one of the top female money-winners in the history of the sport—believes that, in fact, *right*-handers have the advantage. In her book *Bowling*, she maintains that the slight depression on the right side of the lane—if not too extreme—can actually be a help to right-handed bowlers, since it may "guide" the ball to the pins. She also believes that "since fewer people play the left side, there will almost always be more oil there than on the right side. The slicker condition can make it very difficult to throw a good hook ball."

The PBA estimates that approximately 14 or 15 percent of professional bowlers are left-handed.

Some Left-Handed Bowling Greats

Tish Johnson
Dave Davis
Mike Aulby
Steve Cook
Bill Allen
Johnny Petraglia
Patty Costello
Earl Anthony

Boxing

There have been few great left-handed boxers. "Gentleman" Jim Corbett won the world heavyweight crown from John L. Sullivan in New Orleans in 1892, and became the only modern left-handed heavyweight champ. Carmen Basilio—who won the middleweight title in 1957—was also a left-hander, but he boxed right-handed.

In general, left-handers have been ostracized from the ring, and even if they work their way up through the amateur ranks boxing left-handed, they eventually have to learn to fight right-handed to get the pro matches. The reasons for this aren't clear, except that most promoters regard left-handed boxing as dangerous and inequitable, rather like allowing some people to drive on the left side of the road.

Decathlon

In 1976, left-hander Bruce Jenner earned the unofficial title of "World's Greatest Athlete" when he won the gold medal in

Rocky Balboa: The World's Greatest Left-Handed Boxer

Sylvester Stallone was obviously aware of the boxing world's contempt for left-handers when he invented the "Rocky" character.

In the movie *Rocky*, Sylvester Stallone plays Rocky Balboa, a failed left-handed boxer who makes his living breaking arms for a loan shark. When the world champion, Apollo Creed, suddenly finds himself without an opponent for an important match, Rocky becomes the unlikely choice—despite the objection of Apollo Creed's manager, who protests, "I don't want you messin' around with no southpaw." Rocky himself blames his left-handedness for his shabby career when he tells his girl friend, "Nobody wants to fight no southpaw. You know what I mean?"

Rocky does not win the fight (victory is reserved for the film's sequels), but he comes so close to beating the champ that Creed must have rued the day he went "messin' around" with a southpaw. Rocky is a larger-than-life left-handed hero, a likable man who dares to dream the impossible dream and then makes it come true—using the fist that is supposedly his handicap to smash his way to triumph.

the Decathlon at the Montreal Olympics. With his boyish good looks and disarming smile, he captured the imagination of the American public to a degree that was unusual even for an Olympic gold medalist. Soon after the games, he became a commercial spokesman for Wheaties (the "Breakfast of Champions"); later, his fame helped him launch a fledgling movie career, including a role in the less-than-inspired film musical *Can't Stop the Music*, a 1980 "biography" of the disco group the Village People. (Critic Leonard Maltin quipped, "Some people feel they *have* to see what the Village People and Jenner are doing in the same film.")

Jenner was troubled by dyslexia as a child and started playing sports in part to help compensate for problems created by the condition.

Fencing

The Mangiarotti family of Italy was one of the greatest fencing dynasties in the history of the sport. Giuseppe Mangiarotti was a renowned left-handed fencing master in the 1920s. He had three children—two sons and a daughter—all of whom were naturally right-handed. But he taught the daughter and one of the sons, Edoardo, to fence with their left hands, in the belief (confirmed by his own brilliant career) that left-handedness provided a unique advantage in the sport. The results were impressive: Edoardo became a world champion in 1951 and 1954, and was ranked as the most successful fencer of all time. In the 1952 Olympics, Edoardo won the gold medal in fencing; his right-handed brother, Dario, won the silver.

Football

When he was first hoping to make it as a quarterback in the NFL, left-hander Ken Stabler was repeatedly told he had no future in professional football because he threw "with the wrong hand." For many years, there was a widespread prejudice in professional football against left-handed quarterbacks. Some coaches claimed that a left-handed pass was difficult to catch. Others simply didn't like the look of it; they thought it appeared uncoordinated. In reality, the only significant difference between a left-handed quarterback and a right-handed quarterback is that the left-hander's blind side is to his right—a dilemma that is easily solved by beefing up the defense on the right side of the line.

In Stabler's case, the predictions proved premature: he completed almost 60 percent of his passes (for 194 touchdowns) during his professional career, and he led the Oakland Raiders to their 1976 Super Bowl victory.

Some Left-Handed Football Greats

Norman "Boomer" Esiason
Erik Wilhelm
Steve Young
Jim Del Gaizo
David Humm
Paul McDonald

Allie Sherman
Terry Baker
Bobby Douglass
Jim Zorn
Frankie Albert

Golf

"It is better to stand on the wrong side of the ball, and hit it right, than to stand on the right side and hit it wrong."
—Motto of the National Association of Left-Handed Golfers

Of all major sports, golf is probably the most troublesome for a left-handed player. In fact, golfers often joke that left-handers enjoy only one advantage: no one would ever want to steal their clubs.

It's estimated that only about 5 percent of golfers play the game left-handed. No left-handed professional has ever attained the stature of a Snead or a Nicklaus. The high point in left-handed golf came in 1963 when New Zealander Bob Charles became the first left-handed player to win the British Open—a victory assessed by some as "twice as sweet," since it was against Phil Rodgers, a natural left-hander who had long ago chosen to play the game right-handed.

Many natural left-handers become right-handed golfers, some because of the unavailability of left-handed clubs when they first learn to play, others—like champion Ben Hogan—because they are told that left-handers can never be good golfers. Years after he had achieved renown, Hogan regretted having switched. "At that age," he once wrote, "I was gullible enough to believe them and make the change, but I wouldn't now."

Left-handed golf is slowly gaining acceptance, but there still aren't many notable left-handed professionals. Russ Cochran has been a leading money-winner. Phil Mickelson was one of the most promising amateurs of 1991. Bonnie Bryant and Canadian Connie Decker have toured with the LPGA. Bryant, among others, maintains that left-handers should follow their natural bent on the golf course: "If they sweep with a broom as a left-hander, it's a good bet they'll play better golf as a left-hander."

Today, left-handers don't have much trouble getting good clubs. However, some people claim that the architecture of most golf courses still favors right-handed play.

Polo

In 1973, the U.S. Polo Association passed a rule that players meeting head-on must carry the ball on the right side of the pony. Although the rule was instituted strictly for reasons of safety, it effectively banned left-handed play from the sport.

Soccer

Pele (b. 1940)

At one time, Edson Arantes do Nascimento—better known as "Pele"—was arguably the world's most famous left-handed (*and* left-footed) athlete. As the undisputed superstar of the world's most popular sport—international football (or soccer, as it's known in the United States)—he garnered the adoration of millions (especially in his native Brazil), and took home what was once reputed to be the highest salary in sports history. Over a twenty-one-year career, he scored 1,282 goals in 1,364 games and helped the Brazilian national team capture the World Cup three times, in 1958, 1962, and 1970. A 1964 article on his uncanny abilities observed, "Loping or sprinting, he could drag the ball from one foot to the other as if it were a yo-yo on the end of an invisible string . . . intuitively, at any instant, he seemed to know the position of all other players on the field, and to sense just what each man was going to do next."

Unfortunately, as his fame increased so did the enmity of his opponents. Physical attacks against him became commonplace during a game. "Nobody in the game had more fun than I did when I first became a professional," Pele told one magazine. "This honeymoon came to an abrupt end."

After a brief stint playing for the New York Cosmos (for a reported $4.7 million), he retired in 1977.

Tennis

"Weakness turns into strength. It is like a Rommel ambush."
—Rex Lardner *in his book* Finding and Exploiting Your Opponent's Weaknesses, *describing the trap that the right-handed tennis player faces when hitting to a lefty.*

Left-handers enjoy several unique advantages as tennis players:

• Left-handers are said to play a "wristier" game, putting more spin on their serves.

• The spin of the left-hander's shot is the opposite of what the opponent is accustomed to.

• Left-handers are reputed to have powerful forehands.

• Players are trained to hit the ball to the opponent's backhand, normally the weaker left side. But the southpaw's left side is the stronger side.

Sportswriter Rex Lardner offers this pithy assessment of left-handed tennis players: "Left-handers are very offensive-minded. They keep the right-hander off balance because they hit from the wrong side, and they move to the net instinctively to cut off his bewildered returns. They are especially powerful in serving to the ad court and in making slashing crosscourt serve returns from the ad court." The one drawback for left-handers, claims Lardner, is that they have "relatively weak backhands."

Rod "The Rocket" Laver (b. 1938)

In 1962, Australian left-hander Rod Laver became the second man ever to win the Grand Slam of tennis: the Australian, English, French, and U.S. championships in the same year. At 5'8" and 150 pounds, Laver hardly looked like a powerhouse: however, what he lacked in stature he made up for with speed (he could slam the ball with enough force to knock the racket out of an opponent's hand), pinpoint accuracy ("He is the first player," wrote Rex Lardner, "to combine a whipping wrist action with near-perfect control"), and a whirling serve that was difficult to return. In 1969, he won the Grand Slam again, becoming the first player to win it twice. (He also, around this time, became the first tennis professional to earn $1 million.) He capped his career in 1971 by winning thirteen straight matches to capture the Tennis Champions Classic.

Martina Navratilova (b. 1956)

Born and raised in Czechoslovakia, the young Navratilova played in her first tournament when she was eight years old, despite the objections of some officials that she was too small for the courts. By the time she started competing in international tournaments, she was a muscular 5'8" and weighed 140 pounds. She soon made a name for herself with an aggressive net-charging style and a ninety-mile-per-hour serve. Her punishing volleys overpowered most of her opponents. In 1978, she won her first Wimbledon singles title, and for a time she seemed unbeatable, winning six major world championships in a row and setting an all-time record for consecutive match victories (74). She was also the first tennis player to earn $10 million.

In 1975, Navratilova moved from the sports page to the front page when she announced her intention to defect to the United States. She became an American citizen six years later. In the late 1980s, her personal life made headlines, culminating in a much publicized "palimony" suit by former lover Judy Nelson in 1991. The suit was settled out of court.

Jimmy Connors (b. 1952)

"No one's ever given me anything on the court," Jimmy Connors once told an interviewer. "Maybe that's one reason I prefer singles. It's just me and you. When I win, I don't have to congratulate anyone. When I lose, I don't have to blame anyone."

Despite his reputation as a cocky outsider full of disdain for the tennis establishment, Connors has been at the center of professional tennis for two decades. He first learned to play the game from his mother and grandmother, who were both tournament players and who taught him "to be a tiger on the court." Connors started playing professional tennis in 1972, and two years later, with the help of a powerful double-fisted backhand, he won the Australian, the Wimbledon, and the U.S. Open championships. In 1976, he won twelve tournaments, including the U.S. Open, and defeated more than 90 percent of his opponents.

By the early 1980s, with fewer and fewer victories to his credit, Connors was increasingly written off as a has-been by sportswriters. Then he won the Wimbledon in 1982 and the U.S. Open in both 1982 and 1983. Almost a decade later, in 1991—when Connors was approaching forty—he amazed the tennis world by going to the quarterfinals of the U.S. Open. "The secret of Jimmy's big comeback," said his manager, Ray Benton, "is that he never really went away."

Connors seems to have had few problems as a left-hander; in fact, he regards it as a distinct advantage in tennis. He does admit to one difficulty: "When I'm shaking hands, sometimes I put my left hand out. It's tough for me to shake right-handed."

The Davis Cup

In 1900, Dwight F. Davis, an American statesman (and left-hander), founded an international tennis competition between the United States and Europe. In 1902, other nations were invited to join the event, and the Davis Cup became the first truly international tennis competition.

Some Left-Handed Tennis Greats

John McEnroe
Renee Richards
Jaroslav Drobny
Neale Fraser
Art Larsen

Manuel Orantes
Guillermo Villas
Roscoe Tanner
Henri Laconte
Barbara Potter

10

Left-Handers Speak Out

Name: Elizabeth
Age: 37
Profession: Molecular biologist

What, if any, tasks do you perform with the right hand?
"None. I don't favor the right hand in anything."

Is anyone else in your family left-handed?
"My father, and a nephew."

What difficulties have you ever encountered in being left-handed?
"The usual inconveniences. Right-handed desks. I've been told I drive my car very close to the right side of the road; it makes some people very nervous."

Are you aware of any advantages to your left-handedness?
"Supposedly it's easier to open jars left-handed. The muscle groups work better for opening jars."

What kind of grades did you get for penmanship in grade school?
"I don't remember exactly. I had a difficult time with writing. I tried all kinds of different methods: I tried writing backwards,

experimented with different ways to slant the paper, different ways to hold the pen. I had a difficult time understanding how I was supposed to write. The teachers didn't help much."

How would you rate your handwriting now?
"Fair to poor."

Are you artistically inclined?
"In high school, yes. After high school and college, everything got brushed aside. But I loved ceramics and things like that when I was still in school."

Has your left-handedness ever created problems in the workplace?
"I used to deal blackjack to make ends meet when I was an undergraduate in college. The only problem I ever had was once, after I hadn't been dealing for a while, I went back to apply for a job at the Sahara. And I blew it. I got my left hand and my right hand mixed up. I got confused over which end of the table I was supposed to start at, which end you're supposed to start picking up the cards and paying off the players."

Compare your two thumbs. Which thumbnail has the wider and more evenly squared base?
"The left."

Name: John
Age: 45
Profession: Rancher and rodeo rider

Have you ever encountered any prejudice or ridicule because of your left-handedness?
"Only some lighthearted kidding, such as from a friend in college who joked, 'We were all born left-handed, but some of us overcame it.' "

> "I had a job in school at a frozen custard stand. I held the cone in the right hand and scooped the custard with my left. The manager didn't like that. He said I was 'distorting' the custard. So he made me do it the other way."
>
> —Left-hander Bill Neelin, customer service
> representative for Eastman Kodak, 1991

Is anyone else in your family left-handed?

"Some uncles and cousins."

Are you aware of any advantages to your left-handedness?

"In calf roping there's an advantage, because you come up to the calf from your left side. Also, when I was a kid playing Pee-Wee baseball, the coach made me a pitcher because I was left-handed—that only lasted until he discovered I couldn't pitch."

Did anyone ever try to change your handedness?

"In the fourth grade, a teacher tried to force me to write with my right hand, and I was made to stay after school because I refused to do it. Finally, my father—who happened to be the school board president—intervened, which wasn't something he usually did for his children. That was the last I ever heard of having to write right-handed."

What, if any, major tasks do you perform with your right hand?

"A lot of the controls on the equipment I use, like tractors, are right-handed, which forces me to use my right hand quite a bit. I actually do quite a few things with my right hand now because my left wrist has been injured so many times in rodeos."

Do you use any special left-handed equipment for rodeo riding?

"No, not especially. This isn't related to rodeos, but I do own a left-handed bow. And I own a left-handed bolt action rifle."

Compare your two thumbs. Which thumbnail has the wider and more evenly squared base?

"The left, but that's because I slammed the right one in a door. Wait a minute—actually, I think the right one is more evenly squared at the base."

Name: Penny
Age: 45
Profession: Sociologist and educator

Did anyone ever attempt to change your handedness?

"My mother. She tried to get me not to use my left hand. She wanted me to practice everything with the right. I don't think she felt left-handedness was appropriate. A lot of it was appearance-oriented. Sometimes she would even bind my left hand to keep me from using it."

What kind of grades did you get for penmanship in grade school?

"Poor grades. In fact, *very* poor grades. I remember my mother went to a parent-teacher night when I was in the third grade and the teacher suggested I should go to a psychiatrist, my penmanship was such a mess."

How would you rate your handwriting now?

"Legible, though I've had students say they can't read it."

Have you ever had any accidents as a result of being left-handed?

"No. But I have trouble distinguishing the left from the right. Even now, if I'm driving a car and someone says, 'Turn right,' or 'Turn left,' I have to think about it. I'm concerned I may get in an accident simply from getting my directions wrong."

What, if any, major tasks do you perform with your right hand?

"None."

Are you artistically inclined?

"No. Not at all."

Do you tend to make decisions based more on reason and facts or on intuition and emotion?

"On intuition and emotion. Not always. But sometimes I think it'll be my downfall."

Are you aware of any advantages to being left-handed?

"When you have a right-handed lover and you're lying in bed, it works out very well. It's easy to make love to them with your left hand when you're lying on your right side, while they're lying on their left side and making love to you with their right hand. It's a perfect fit."

Compare your two thumbs. Which thumbnail has the wider and more evenly squared base?

"The left."

"I can see the day when a ninety-degree angle is known as a 'left' angle; when a moral, virtuous person will be called 'lefteous'; and when a box standing on its bottom will be 'upleft.' "

—Customer at a Westport, Connecticut, specialty shop for left-handers, 1977

Name: Mark
Age: 26
Profession: Male stripper

What, if any, difficulties have you ever encountered in being left-handed?

"I always get put at the end of the table at family dinners. My uncle jokes that I wasn't really born left-handed, that I became that way so I could meet girls—rubbing elbows and all that at restaurant counters. I have to remind him that, given what I do for a living, I don't exactly have a problem meeting *lots* of women."

Have you ever had any other difficulties?

"Scissors, spiral notebooks. Lots of small things. I'm sure you've heard all this before. I haven't used a power saw since I was a teenager, but I remember being scared to death I was going to cut all my fingers off."

What about in your profession, the fact that most men's clothes are designed for right-handers?

"Most of the outfits I wear when I'm performing have Velcro 'breakaways.' I do everything else with my right hand when I'm onstage."

Is anyone else in your family left-handed?

"No. I had an aunt who was a dancer. She was right-handed; I think she did everything with her right hand. But she always used to say, 'I must've been born left-handed. You know, I really think I'm left-handed.' She didn't have any particular reason for it—none that I knew of anyway. She just always insisted that she'd been born left-handed. She'd try to write with her left hand sometimes, and it always looked like gibberish."

Are you aware of any advantages to your left-handedness?

"It's an icebreaker sometimes. I'll be signing autographs and

> "I always felt special being left-handed. I always thought it was a special gift. I figured all sensitive and creative people were left-handed."
>
> —Artist Susan Rios, 1991

someone will say, 'Oh, you're left-handed!' Women seem to think it's cute."

Have you ever had any accidents as a result of being left-handed?
"No."

Did anyone ever attempt to change your handedness?
"No."

Have you ever had any problems with dyslexia or stuttering?
"No. I'm not a very good speller, though."

Compare your two thumbs. Which thumbnail has the wider and more evenly squared base?
"The left. Definitely the left."

Name: Peter
Age: 24
Profession: Book editor

Are you aware of any advantages to your left-handedness?
"Tollbooths are designed for left-handers. I do think being left-handed affects the way that you think and solve problems. I personally believe left-handed people are more creative."

Have you ever encountered any prejudice or ridicule over being left-handed?

"Not prejudice or ridicule exactly. People are often amazed at how I write. I hold my paper sideways so it almost looks as if I'm writing upside down sometimes."

What difficulties, if any, have you ever encountered in being left-handed?
"I can't write with a fountain pen. There was never a left-handed glove for playing softball in gym class at school."

Is anyone else in your family left-handed?
"No."

What was your parents' reaction to your left-handedness?
"When I was an infant I kept picking up the spoon with my left hand. My mother told me, 'No!' and put it in my right hand. She finally gave up after a while."

What kind of grades did you get for penmanship in school?
"B's."

What, if any, problems did you have in school as a result of being left-handed?
"If I ever used any kind of smearable ink, I'd get it all over my hand, because I'd always wind up dragging my hand through whatever I'd written. And of course the right-handed desks were impossible."

Compare your two thumbs. Which thumbnail has the wider and more evenly squared base?
"The left."

What, if any, major tasks do you perform with your right hand?
"I play certain sports—squash, tennis, golf—right-handed. At

some point, I finally learned how to use a pair of scissors with my right hand. Other than that I do almost everything else left-handed; brush my teeth, throw a ball, things like that."

Name: Margaret
Age: 77
Profession: Poet

Have you ever had any accidents as a result of being left-handed?
"None that I can think of."

What, if any, difficulties have you ever encountered in being left-handed?
"Everything is made for right-handed people, but you get used to that. In a restaurant, the waitresses always put things— the water glass, the check, et cetera—on the wrong side. Also, scissors: right-handed scissors bruise my hands."

Do you perform any major tasks with your right hand?
"Just ironing."

Did anyone ever attempt to change your handedness?
"No, not that I recall."

Compare your two thumbs. Which thumbnail has the wider and more evenly squared base?
"My left."

Are you aware of any advantages to being left-handed?
"No—but then, I can't think of any advantage it would be to be right-handed."

Name: Stan
Age: 56
Profession: Woodworker

Have you ever encountered any prejudice or ridicule over your left-handedness?

"No, but by the time I was in eighth grade I was five-ten and weighed one hundred and eighty pounds. You don't get too much ridicule when you're built like that."

Have you ever encountered any problems in your profession because of being left-handed?

"No. I don't find too many problems with tools. Like with a Skilsaw—it's made for right-handed use, but I'm so used to using it right-handed after all these years that I don't have any problems with it. Likewise, a table saw. I think most left-handers learn to become somewhat ambidextrous."

> "We no longer want to be 'left' out, 'left' behind, 'left' over, put out in 'left' field, or given any 'left'-handed compliments. Most important, we want society to realize that left-handers have special needs and shouldn't be forced to conform to the world of right-handers."
>
> —Jancy Campbell, executive director of Lefthanders International, 1977

Did anyone ever attempt to change your handedness?

"They *did* change it, when I was in first grade. They made me learn to write right-handed. And I think it made me nervous. I had ulcers by the time I was thirteen, and I'm not an ulcer-type person. I think the change screws you up. I have problems telling left from right, clockwise from counterclockwise."

Any other problems in school?

"Desks. I had problems with the right-handed desks. Also, even though I wrote on paper with my right hand, I still wrote on the blackboard with my left hand—that always drew a lot of comment. All through high school, I was a straight-A student, but I drank heavily. Whether the drinking had anything to do with being left-handed, I'm not sure. I always wondered if it did."

Is anyone else in your family left-handed?

"No."

Have you ever had any accidents as a result of being left-handed?

"Near-accidents. When I'm in a car and somebody says, 'Turn left,' 'Go right,' I have to stop and think about it. I've had some close calls."

Are you artistically inclined?

"Not with a paintbrush or anything like that, but with wood, yes. I can visualize what a project will look like even before it's done, and most other people can't. I have a strong spatial sense. But then working with wood *is* working with space."

Compare your two thumbs. Which thumbnail has the wider and more evenly squared base?

"The right, I think. But then the left one has been beat up and scarred so many times, it's hard to tell. But I'd say the right."

Name: Patricia
Age: 46
Profession: Public relations assistant at
the National Baseball Hall of Fame and Museum

Is anyone else in your family left-handed?

"My brother—who's an architect, by the way. Also, my father's sister. And one of my three daughters. I have mixed feelings about my daughter being left-handed. In a way, I'm proud, but a little bit sorry she has to contend with a lot of the things left-handers face."

Did anyone ever attempt to change your handedness?

"I was never *forced* to change, but my father was annoyed that my brother and I were left-handed. He encouraged us to try things right-handed. He had a sister who was left-handed. The family went to extreme lengths to try and change *her*, including tying her hand behind her back. To this day, she still stutters. My mother had a hard time watching me do household tasks left-handed. She'd say, 'I *can't* watch you peel carrots. It looks so awkward.' It's kind of difficult growing up when people tell you how awkward you are."

Have you ever encountered any prejudice or ridicule because of your left-handedness?

"Oh, I got picked on a little in school; everyone would call me 'Lefty.' It still gets commented on. On the other hand, other

"It happens all the time. A guy will come up to me in a bar or somewhere and say, 'Hey, Ken, I'm a left-hander, too.' And it means something to me. I don't care how obnoxious he might be. I think, hey, maybe he's not such a bad Joe. There's a bond there."

—Left-handed football pro Ken Stabler, 1977

left-handers will say things to me like, 'I *knew* I liked something about you.'

How would you rate your handwriting?
"Not bad, though everything I write goes uphill."

Are you artistically inclined?
"I'm good at decorating, using colors."

Compare your two thumbs. Which thumbnail has the wider and more evenly squared base?
"My right."

Name: Gene
Age: 34
Profession: Free-lance writer

Is anyone else in your family left-handed?
"An aunt and my grandfather, both on my father's side."

What, if any, major tasks do you perform with your right hand?
"Lots of things. I switch back and forth between my hands all the time, without thinking. Sometimes I eat left-handed, sometimes I eat right-handed—things like that. I was playing miniature golf recently, and I got through the first hole before I suddenly realized I was playing *left*-handed. The few times I'd

played before that, it was always right-handed. I didn't even notice at first. With miniature golf clubs, you don't notice much difference. But for a moment I was standing there getting really confused: 'Which side am I *supposed* to swing from?' "

What difficulties have you ever encountered in being left-handed?

"I can never remember which way to deal cards, clockwise or counterclockwise. If anyone even uses the terms 'clockwise' or 'counterclockwise,' I have to visualize a clock in my mind and then think carefully to remember which way the hands turn."

Have you ever had any accidents as a result of being left-handed?

"No, nothing I can think of."

Can you read backwards easily?

"Yes. Backwards and upside down. The few times I've done it, though, it leaves me feeling unhinged, as if my brain's being pulled apart. I have a friend who can do it really easily too, and he says that it always leaves him feeling as if he's popped into an alternate dimension for a few minutes."

Did anyone ever try to change your handedness?

"Not that I can remember. I don't think my mother was very happy about my being left-handed, though. She'd always say, 'You must've gotten that from your father's side of the family.' She didn't think it looked 'proper' to be left-handed. To this day I think she's somewhat disappointed in me because of it."

Compare your two thumbs. Which thumbnail has the wider and more evenly squared base?

"The right."

"I can still remember the crisis I created in third grade when I insisted on saluting the flag with my left hand. I've no doubt some whey-faced sleuth opened a dossier on me at that very time, one that must now occupy several filing cabinets and contain all manner of damning information about my persistent portsidedness. If you think I exaggerate the bias against us left-handers, trying raising your *left* hand the next time you bear witness in a court of law."

—Author Richard Starnes, 1976

Name: Bob
Age: 59
Profession: Software design engineer

What kind of grades did you get for penmanship in grade school?
"Between an F and F-minus. When I was in the fourth grade, they gave up and I started using a typewriter."

How would you rate your handwriting now?
"Nonexistent."

Did anyone ever attempt to change your handedness?
"No, which might be surprising given the era in which I was raised."

What, if any problems, did you have in school as a result of being left-handed?
"The typical ones. The inkwell was on the wrong side of the desk, that sort of thing."

Are you aware of any advantages to your left-handedness?
"Being extremely intelligent and creative. And of course being *very* modest. Actually, I *do* think there is a correlation, particu-

larly in the creative side of things. I can write upside down and backwards—if you can call that an advantage really. I can also read things upside down and backwards that *other people* have written: things lying on their desks, for example. I can read them just as smoothly as if they were right side up to me."

Have you ever had any accidents as a result of being left-handed?

"Once when I was in a hurry I ran into a door that had IN printed on the *other* side of the glass. I broke two ribs. If there are letters printed on a glass door, I never know which side of the door I'm on."

Looking at signs, posters, or other printed material, do you ever find yourself transposing or rearranging letters or words just for the fun of it?

"Constantly. I tend with very short words to read them from right to left anyway. When I see a sign on the road that says POTS, I know to stop. I know that when you have indigestion, you're supposed to reach for SMUT. If I'm listening to someone just babbling on and I'm not really paying attention, I'll start rearranging the letters and words on book titles or posters, just to amuse myself."

Is anyone else in your family left-handed?

"No."

What, if any, major tasks do you perform with your right hand?

"I saw with my right hand. Brush my teeth right-handedly. Also kick with my right foot. I can also write with my right hand, but it doesn't get much practice."

Compare your two thumbs. Which thumbnail has the wider and more evenly squared base?

"I can't tell any difference. They look the same to me."

"When I was a kid I seemed to do everything back to front. I used to write backwards, and every time the masters at my school looked at my book, they used to throw little fits. I had difficulties outside school, too. I couldn't learn to ride a bike because I would insist on pedaling backwards and was quite convinced that mine was the right way, and everybody else's was wrong. I do everything with my left hand, and no matter how hard I try I can't alter the habit. A doctor once told me I shouldn't try to, because being left-handed is something to do with the brain."

—Singer Paul McCartney

Name: George
Age: 44
Profession: Agricultural consultant and feed broker

Did anyone ever attempt to change your left-handedness?

"No. My older brother was left-handed, but he was switched to right-handed writing in school. I think my parents saw the problems he had and decided it wasn't a very good idea."

Is anyone else in your family left-handed?

"My maternal grandmother."

What kind of grades did you get for penmanship in grade school?

"Not good. Not good at all. It didn't seem fair somehow to be graded on penmanship. I was a really good student. I used to take the report card home and my mother and I would always bemoan the C's in penmanship."

What, if any, problems did you have in school as a result of being left-handed?

"Just the usual—the inconvenience of spiral notebooks and

right-handed desks. Shop class was a mess if you were left-handed. I did have a speech problem when I was a child. I had a problem pronouncing consonants and had to go to a speech therapist. Everyone said I sounded like a Southerner. I don't know if that was related to being left-handed, though."

Are you artistically inclined?
"No. In fact, I have a great deal of trouble drawing any kind of figures. I doodle a lot, but I don't draw figures when I doodle. I doodle words, over and over again."

What, if any, major tasks do you perform with your right hand?
"I usually open things with my right hand. It seems much easier. There aren't many things I do with my right hand otherwise."

Compare your two thumbs. Which thumbnail has the wider and more evenly squared base?
"The right one is wider, but the left one is more evenly squared."

Name: Fred
Age: 56
Profession: Psychiatrist

Is anyone else in your family left-handed?
"Three of my brothers—out of eleven kids, four of us wound up being left-handed. One of my sons is left-handed. Also, my wife."

Did anyone ever attempt to change your handedness?
"I was born and raised in the Philippines, and the nuns where I went to school switched me to right-handed penmanship. I still write with my right hand; though if I'm on the phone and holding the receiver right-handed, I'll sometimes just pick up a pen

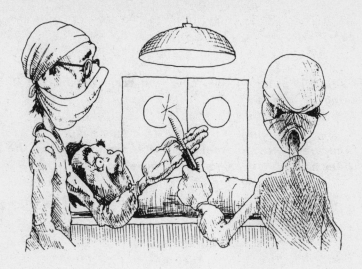

and write down a phone number or whatever with my left hand rather than switch the phone."

What other major tasks do you perform with your right hand?

"I suture and use a scalpel with my right hand. But I use surgical scissors with my left. I eat with my right hand, brush my teeth with my right hand. Everything else I do left-handed."

In your professional life, have you ever seen clients whose problems were related to being left-handed?

"Yes, in the sense that some left-handers have problems with dyslexia, those kinds of things."

How easy is it to treat dyslexia?

"Very. In fact, my left-handed son had some problems with dyslexia. I had one of his teachers cut the letters of the alphabet out of sandpaper. Then I'd have him gently run his hands over the shape of each letter, to *feel* them. We used other teaching aids to help train his eye movements for reading. Within six months, the problem was resolved. He loves to read now, is very well-read. In fact, most of his money goes for books and music."

What difficulties, if any, have you ever encountered in being left-handed?
"I can't think of any."

Compare your two thumbs. Which thumbnail has the wider and more evenly squared base?
"They're the same. The left might be a little bit wider."

Name: Susan
Age: 49
Profession: Registered dietitian

Is anyone else in your family left-handed?
"My mother, and one of my uncles. Two nieces. Also, my ex-husband."

What kind of grades did you get for penmanship in grade school?
"Fine. In fact, I have very neat handwriting. However, I 'hook' when I write, and when I was a science teacher I found it very difficult to write on the blackboard. My writing looked very primitive. You can't 'hook' very well on a chalkboard."

How did the students react to your left-handedness?
"The left-handed students tended to react very positively."

What, if any, major tasks do you perform with your right hand?
"I use scissors with my right hand. When I was a little girl, I tried using scissors left-handed; but in the third grade I got so frustrated trying to cut snowflakes out of folded paper that I

> "I am left-handed. It isn't my fault. I was born that way. But as a small boy I was punished for it because my schoolmasters thought it was a deliberate perversity. I tried and cried. Scrawls and smudges on the paper: and, when the master wasn't looking, back went the pen into my left hand because *that was natural for me.*"
>
> —Rev. Mervyn Stockwood,
> Bishop of Southwark, 1963

made the switch. I do pretty much everything else with my left hand."

What difficulties have you ever encountered in being left-handed?

"I've taken classes where I've been at large lecture halls and the only left-handed desks are invariably in the back row. Also, because I 'hook,' I have problems with notebooks with the metal spiral on top. Usually I just turn the tablet upside down, so the spiral's on the bottom."

Compare your two thumbs. Which thumbnail has the wider and more evenly squared base?

"I think maybe the right. But they look pretty similar."

Name: Lisa
Age: 14
Profession: Freshman in high school

Is anyone else in your family left-handed?

"Just my older sister. My younger sister, both of my parents, and all four of my grandparents are right-handed."

What kind of grades did you get for penmanship in grade school?

"All A's."

> "All left-handed people feel awkward, but they think *they're* clumsy when actually they don't have the proper tools. For example, you really have to take off a watch to wind it properly. When I park a car, I can parallel park better on the left side than on the right side. Even though many left-handers are seemingly ambidextrous, it is difficult to tell which hand they favor except when they light a match. You can always tell if a person is left-handed by the way he lights a match."
> —June Gittleson, proprietor of The Left
> Hand, a New York specialty store, 1974

Did any of your teachers give you any kind of special advice or guidance on how to write left-handed?
"No. I was on my own."

Did anyone ever attempt to change your handedness?
"No."

Do they provide you with a left-handed desk at school?
"No. All the desks are the same. They're square-shaped, neither left- nor right-handed."

Do you excel in any sports?
"Basketball and track. I can dribble with my left hand, and I shoot baskets left-handed. It gives me an advantage. Most players are used to people dribbling with their right hands, so when they try to block me it's always on the right side; I just go around the other way."

What, if any, major tasks do you perform with your right hand?
"None."

Have you ever encountered any difficulties in being left-handed?
"No."

Are you aware of any advantages, other than in basketball, to your left-handedness
 "Not really. It doesn't really matter that much."

Compare your two thumbs. Which thumbnail has the wider and more evenly squared base?
 "The right."

11

Left-Handers' Resources

Books

Several years ago, veteran sports announcer Vin Scully—a left-hander—publicly swore off how-to guides on golf. "It drove me crazy trying to figure out what those books were talking about," he said. Unfortunately, many general guide books—for golf, tennis, needlepoint, calligraphy, etc.—are almost useless to left-handers, since the instructions are almost always written exclusively for right-handed readers. In her book *Tennis to Win*, Billie Jean King sanguinely advises left-handed readers simply to "think 'left' when I write 'right,' and vice versa." It doesn't always work. The books listed below are either written especially for left-handed readers or include good sections on left-handed aspects of their subject matter. Beyond this list, it always pays to browse through secondhand bookstores for other titles that may be of interest to left-handers.

Also, some mail-order firms have occasionally published their own guide books or pamphlets (for example, Lefthanders International puts out books on left-handed knitting and crochet). Always be sure to ask what specific titles they offer.

GENERAL INTEREST

Left-Handed People by Michael Barsley
Lefties by Jack Fincher
The Natural Superiority of the Left-Hander by James De Kay
The Power of Your Other Hand: A Course in Channelling the Inner Wisdom of the Right Brain by Lucia Capacchione
Sinister People by Jack Fincher
The World's Greatest Left-Handers by James De Kay and Sandy Huffaker

TENNIS

Finding and Exploiting Your Opponent's Weaknesses by Rex Lardner
Advanced Tennis by Paul Metzler
Sinister Tennis by Peter Schwed

GOLF

Left Hander's Golf Book by Earl Stewart, Jr., and Dr. Harry E. Gunn
The Bob Charles Left-hander's Golf Book by Bob Charles with Jim Wallace
Golf from the Other Side (video) by Bob Charles

SPECIAL INTEREST

Left-Handed Guitar by Nicholas Clarke
Left-Handed Calligraphy by Vance Studley
Left-Handed Stitchery by Sally Cowan
Teaching Left-Handed Children by Margaret M. Clark

CHILDREN'S

The Story of Left-Handedness by Marguerite Rush Lerner

Organizations

Lefthanders International, Inc.
P.O. Box 8249
Topeka, Kansas 66608
(913) 234-2177

National Association of Left-Handed Golfers
P.O. Box 801223
Houston, Texas 77280-1223
(713) 464-8683

Sinistral SIG
200 Emmett Avenue
Derby, Connecticut 06418
(203) 735-1759
A left-handers' interest group of Mensa.

Retail Outlets and Mail-Order Suppliers for Left-Handed Merchandise

Left Hand Solutions and Registry, Inc.
P.O. Box 617
Port Jefferson Station, New York 11776
(516) 474-0091
(800) 649-5338 (in-state calls only)

Catalog and mail-order supplier of left-handed tools, utensils, and other merchandise of interest to left-handers. Publishes and sells *The Left-Hander's Guide and Reference Manual* by John Diana (which includes lengthy how-to sections on left-handed bowling, golf, tennis, and baseball). Also compiles and acts as a clearinghouse for questionnaire information (family histories, medical information, personal histories) on left-handers.

Lefthanders International, Inc.
P.O. Box 8249
Topeka, Kansas 66608
(913) 234-2177

Catalog and mail-order supplier of left-handed tools, utensils, and other merchandise of interest to left-handers. Also publishes *Lefthander* magazine (bimonthly).

The Sinister Shop
P.O. Box 261, Station C
Toronto MGJ2P4
Canada
(416) 366-1790

Catalog and mail-order supplier of left-handed tools, utensils, and other merchandise of interest to left-handers.

Left Hand World
P.O. Box 330128
Pier 39
San Francisco, California 94133-0128
(415) 433-3547
Retail store.

Handtiques
6072 Busch Boulevard
Columbus, Ohio 43229
(614) 846-0778
Retail store.

Lefties Corner
508 Monroe
Detroit, Michigan 48226
(313) 964-5123
Retail store.

Lefties Corner
39 Jackson Street
Indianapolis, Indiana 46225
(317) 631-5505
Retail store.

Fry's Left-Handers Supply
P.O. Box 19, Country Ridge
Melissa, Texas 75071
(214) 871-0719
Retail store and mail order.

Check your local phone book for other left-handers' stores that may operate in your city or town.